To Karen Randall,
Wishing you happy holidays all year long —

Rebecca Johnston

Hometown Holidays
Memories Throughout The Year

Jones Mercantile Co. decorated for Christmas in 1957.
Photo courtesy of Cherokee County Historical Society

Rebecca Johnston

Copyright 2008 by Rebecca Johnston

Hometown Holidays
Published by Yawn's Publishing
210 East Main Street
Canton, GA 30114
www.yawnsbooks.com

All rights reserved. No part of this book may be reproduced or transmitted in any form, electronic or mechanical, including photocopying, recording, or data storage systems without the express written permission of the publisher, except for brief quotations in reviews and articles.

ISBN13: 978-0-9818673-1-1
ISBN10: 0-9818673-1-6

Printed in the United States

Table of Contents

Christmas	5
New Year's Day	47
Valentine's Day	55
Easter	73
Mother's Day	89
Father's Day	103
Fourth of July	111
Halloween	123
Thanksgiving	133

Acknowledgements

I dedicate this book to my family. First and foremost to my husband Harry, my son Nathan, daughter-in-law Katie and daughter Ann who are the center of my life, around which everything else rotates. To my parents, Jim and Vern Wheeler, who gave me so much love and left me with so many happy memories. Thanks to my sister Carole Ann and brother Jim Jr. and my grandmother, Belle Cochran Wheeler, whom we always called Gran, for all the good times we shared in childhood.

Thanks to all my friends who have indulged me in allowing me to write about our lives together and who have given me support and advice. Thanks to all those at the Cherokee Tribune, who for so many years have been like my second family.

Thanks to fellow columnist Juanita Hughes and to my friends at the Cherokee County Historical Society for their help and support in compiling this book.

Most especially, thanks to you, all the readers of the Cherokee Tribune and my column over the years, who have let me know when you liked what I wrote, and sometimes when you didn't. Your input and support are invaluable.

Christmas

Rebecca helps decorate her family Christmas tree.

"I will honor Christmas in my heart and try to keep it all the year."
　　　　　　　　　　Charles Dickens

Christmas Comes From the Heart

Seeing the lights of Christmas trees twinkling from the windows of houses which the rest of the year are curtained and closed is one of my favorite sights this special holiday.

Each family's tradition is different. I have one neighbor who like clockwork puts up her decorations on Thanksgiving evening and takes them down the minute Christmas is past.

One home on Main Street features a large tree with colored lights which is the first thing I see as I round the corner toward town. It shines through sheer curtains which the rest of the year are opaque.

Another home has a shimmering tree in the sunroom on the side of the house which is visible from a long distance down the street.

Some homes offer only tantalizing glimpses of their holiday trees, while others are totally revealed in their entire splendor.

My grandmother, whom some of you may remember as Gran, never had a Christmas tree or any other Christmas decorations that I can remember in all the years she and I enjoyed together, but her home radiated the true Christmas spirit.

Perhaps when she was younger and had small children of her own the family home was decorated for the holidays, but by the time I was born she was almost 70 years old and had ceased with the commercial trappings of Christmas.

Instead, she immersed herself in the religious celebrations, a tradition she continued all year long.

This was a lady who did not even play cards – or our favorite game of dominoes – on Sunday. She read her Bible everyday, went to church every service, always sitting on her same pew, and listened to the religious programs on the radio.

Her other pursuits included reading the North Georgia Tribune, forerunner of this newspaper, talking with her friends on the telephone and keeping house.

She never drove a car, never owned a television set or worked outside the home. She did make all her own clothes, stay in touch with family and friends far away by mail, keep house until she was in her 90s and try to teach me to be a kinder and sweeter person. She also lavished love on her family, especially me.

Basically she spoiled me rotten, or so my husband still sometimes complains.

Gran has been dead for more than a decade, but hardly a day goes by that I do not think fondly of her, and especially at the holidays, memories of her come flooding back.

Even though the normal trappings of Christmas as we know them were absent from her home, a truer peace was always present.

Whatever she had, and sometimes it was very little, she would gladly share with others. Every gift she ever received was welcomed with true joy.

I can remember how thrilled she was with the divinity candy brought by her good neighbor Mrs. Henderson, and the joy she got from a potted plant a group of young people from the church gave her. Each gift was proudly displayed and shared with others who came by.

Each Christmas card she got during the holidays was set on the mantle to remind us of the season. Sometimes we would get out old scrapbooks of Christmas cards sent to her by my father and aunt from Europe and postings in the states during World War II and pore over the elaborate greetings or the single pages of holiday messages on thin airmail paper.

Her life spanned almost a century, including two world wars and thousands of happy, sad and bittersweet memories.

To walk into her living room was to walk into a world where time stood still, where the harsher realities of life were kept at bay by an abiding faith in God and love of her fellow man.

Seeing Christmas trees shining forth fills me with joy of the holiday season, but memories of my Gran give me a special Christmas feeling.

We can hang all the tinsel, and decorate the tree, and buy expensive gifts, but the true meaning of Christmas is something that can only be found in the heart.

Dreams of Christmas Past

Christmas memories swirl like snowflakes softly falling on a winter night.

They come down so gently, touching my face before melting away into the shadows of times past.

I see my father standing over a big wooden bowl of walnuts, breaking their shells with an old nutcracker. He takes out the nutmeat and hands it to us children before eating any himself.

He looks at us and laughs as we grab the nuts and dance off, his eyes sparkling and his cheeks rosy with the joys of Christmas.

I see my mother mixing the cornbread dressing, stirring up a wonderful Christmas dinner for her family, seasoning everything she cooks with love and care. She never smiles as much as my dad, but in her hands and her work she gives of herself to her family.

I see us in our living room as twilight falls on Christmas Eve, my younger brother and sister and me gathered on the floor by the brightly lit tree, looking up through the branches gleaming with icicles and colored lights.

We dream of presents and fun and wishes come true. We fight among ourselves, but in good humor, slapping each other's hands when we reach out to tear a corner off the colored wrappings of the packages. We vow to tell on one another, not really meaning it, then turn over on our backs and look up through the boughs of the Christmas tree.

Darkness comes down to cloak our house, the pine trees outside lined against the purple night sky like mighty firs at the North Pole.

We stand at the picture window, pressing our noses against the cold panes, looking out for Santa Claus, straining to see him in the gloom of winter night.

Our parents come in and hand us our stockings, glittery with our names, furry and red. They draw us back into the warmth of the room, as they help us hang them above the fireplace. We put a little plate of cookies on the cold hearth, along with a glass of milk, in anticipation of Santa.

Then we all sit down, fighting over who gets to sit where, and read "The Night Before Christmas" out of the tattered little book, taking turns, almost reciting the familiar pages.

My father gets out the family Bible and we listen to him read us the real Christmas story, the ageless message cloaked in ancient language.

My brother wiggles away, grabbing the little figures out of the manger scene, becoming restless, fueled by too much sugar and Christmas cookies.

My mother goes back into the kitchen to put the finishing touches on things there. My father reaches over and gives us each a big hug or pats us on our heads, depending on how still we are for that moment.

Every Christmas of my childhood is the same tableaux: family traditions layered on one by one and repeated each holiday season until they become the standard fare of our celebration.

They comfort us and draw us together as a family when we are one, but as we grow apart, leave home and change through the fleeting years and seasons, those same traditions and memories weave together to become the stuff of Christmas past.

They remain somewhere deep within us always, rising up at unexpected moments out of the dark recesses of our memories.

The sparkle of a shiny ornament, the smell of gingerbread, the shape of a tree conjures up the magic that was childhood, a time when we felt safe and secure.

No matter where our lives take us, no matter how many years pass, we always have our memories. We pass the traditions on to our children and they treasure them as much as we did.

Once more I'm back in my childhood memory, feeling the cold of the window pane on my forehead as I try to see out into the Christmas night.

My sister comes up and grabs my hand and tells me it's time for bed. We run together into our bedroom, jumping into the bed together, pulling up the covers.

I close my eyes and in what seems only a flash I wake up to the light of a new morning. And it's Christmas.

Savoring Joys of Giving

Christmas gift!

That's what my father always called out on Christmas morning and how my grandmother answered the telephone on Christmas Day when I called her house to tell her we were coming to get her so she could see what we got from Santa.

Of course, we had already called the radio station to tell the whole community what was under our tree. That was a huge Canton custom in those days, and my grandmother, who never owned a television, would sit in her rocking chair in the front bedroom and listen eagerly to her little radio all morning to hear us and all our friends call in.

An important part of the holidays is gift giving, and I think I am like most people when I say that the fun of Christmas is in buying presents for those I love, appreciate and care about. The true meaning is of course the birth of One who came to save all of us. But the Wise Men started a custom that has certainly stood the test of time, too.

It's not so much what I get, although my family will tell you I love presents. It's about what I choose and give to others. The fun of finding just that right item for my brother, something he has wanted all year, and wrapping it up and putting it under the tree. Or looking for something I know my mother will really, really like.

Rebecca Johnston

I remember those days when my children were little and every year there was one toy that everyone just had to have. We would call relatives in faraway states, in hopes that the craze hadn't reached that far. It always had. We would camp out at unheard-of hours at the discount stores waiting for a new toy shipment. Cabbage Patch kids, Holiday Barbies, Star Wars figures and others that have passed into toy oblivion.

When I was a child, Christmas was a more simple time. Everyone decorated for about a week, and there were usually only one or two gifts for each person under the tree.

One year I got a bicycle, perhaps my favorite gift ever. I remember my father standing in his suit and hat on Christmas afternoon helping me learn to ride in the Jones Mercantile parking lot where the Cherokee County Justice Center stands today.

Another year it was a dollhouse, one of those metal Colonial structures that looked like the house where "My Three Sons" lived.

And then when I was about eight or nine, Barbie was born. For the rest of my childhood my Christmas wish list was comprised of the outfits I wanted for Barbie. We didn't expect to get a new doll every year. We were lucky if we had a Ken and Midge doll to hang out with Barbie

What we wanted was the wedding dress, the black slinky evening gown, the garden party outfit, the flight attendant uniform and the tennis dress. I kept all my outfits stored in a black plastic truck that was my treasure trove of the imagination.

When I was about 10 years old I had my first real experience of the thrill of buying a gift for someone else that I hoped would delight her.

I think we children were each given about $10 or so by our parents to go shop in downtown Canton.

After a stroll past the Santa and bears and elves in the windows of Jones Mercantile Store and a perusal of the dusting powders and colognes in Canton Drug Store for my mother and grandmother, I headed to the king of Canton dime stores, Kessler's.

After a quick glance at the 45s, I headed downstairs to the toy section. And there I found a wooden baby doll crib that rocked and that I could afford. I think it cost about three dollars. I was so proud of that toy, I could hardly wait until my little sister opened it on Christmas morning and I could see her delight with my gift. I don't know whether she even remembers it, but it has always stood out in my memory.

As much fun as toys and presents are at Christmas, giving of ourselves is of course the most meaningful present.

As I got older, going to Coker Nursing Home to sing carols or packing a box with food and clothes for a family in need became a highlight of my holidays. Saving a part of my allowance for the Christmas offering at church or pinching pennies to buy a doll or game for a child who had less became more of what Christmas really meant.

This week I watched a carload of young girls, possibly a Scout troop, tumble happily out of a car at the assisted living home where my mother now resides. I looked at the glow in their faces and heard the joy in their voices, and I thought about all the happiness they would share with the residents inside.

I saw volunteers at MUST ministries in Canton unloading carloads of donated gifts and food at the back loading dock, and I saw young mothers with small children and elderly folks lining up at the front door to find Christmas for their families.

I saw signs all around town of neighbors helping neighbors, people reaching out to others.

I felt the joy of giving in the air, and I thought "Christmas gift."

Spirit of Patriotism Colors Holiday

The year of 2001 will go down in my record book as the year of exuberant decorating.

Local retailers report brisk sales on holiday decorations such as trees, garlands, ornaments and lights. Lots and lots and lots of lights.

Lights are everywhere you turn. Hung from shrubbery, dangling on the eves of houses, springing up on lawns. Forests of spiral trees dot the landscape, and herds of gaily-lit deer leap across yards.

I don't think any of this is a coincidence. In the face of war, in the aftermath of a tragedy that brought death and destruction into our midst, we are sending a message out into the world. We are once more bravely lighting the American candle to say the spirit of our country will never be extinguished.

I don't think any Christmas tree will be without a symbol of patriotism this holiday season. The most popular items are now Christmas decorations in the red, white and blue color scheme. Drive by the windows of Canton Florist and take a look at the beautiful tree done all in red, white and blue. And many homeowners are following suit.

Cars and trucks displaying flags are now adding a bit of holiday greenery and a bow to the front of their vehicle. America is in the holiday spirit.

Maybe we're spending a little less this year, maybe we are buying fewer gifts, but we are all

Rebecca Johnston

drawing a little closer to the true meaning of Christmas. We are all taking a few moments to realize a little bit more what is really important in our lives.

Growing up as a child in the 1960s in Canton, decorating our homes was a much simpler process. Maybe it was the same for you. We had a tree, a wreath on the door and a crèche or manger scene prominently displayed in the living room.

Decorating the tree was done one week before Christmas Day. We would get out the boxes of ornaments, the strings of colored lights and the silver icicles and begin the job that always included the whole family and sometimes some friends.

The most important job was putting the icicles on the tree. You know, those little thin ones that came in boxes. We would string them strand by strand all over the tree until in our eyes it positively glowed.

Another tradition at our house was the Storybook dolls, those small dolls dressed as the characters of fairy tales and children's stories. We had Snow White and Cinderella, Sleeping Beauty and the Bride doll. We tucked them into the branches of the tree.

Those dolls were gifts to my sister and me from Mr. Louis Jones, president of the Canton Textile Mills. He would give them as gifts to many of the ladies who worked at the mill office, and because my father worked there too, we were included. We loved those dolls, even though we weren't allowed to play with them and they only came out of their boxes once a year.

My father always took great delight in Christmas. He loved receiving greeting cards and would read each one with delight. The holiday cookies and candies and treats were eagerly devoured. My memories are of laughter and love and light.

We always had a live green tree. My mother would make the wreath on the door out of holly that grew in our yard and the woods around our house.

Some of my friends with more modern parents had those silver trees that didn't have any lights on them, but had a little spotlight and a color wheel that turned, shining on the tree and turning it green then red then blue in turn.

One of my favorite trees was at my friend Jeannie's. It was a flocked tree, a real evergreen turned snow white with snowy spray paint, and decorated all in red - red ornaments and red lights. It always dazzled me.

In those days, we all held dear to our individual family traditions. We took them out each year and touched them and felt them and allowed them to fill our homes and our lives with the special warmth of Christmas. They brought us comfort and hope and joy, just like the spirit of the first Christmas.

This holiday season, the colors of Christmas are mixed into palettes of patriotism.

So let's light a special light for peace, for the prayer that terrorism will be subdued, that the families who have been touched most closely with this tragedy will find a renewed message in the season.

Let's take time to remember.

Saying Good-Bye at Christmastime

Many of you know that last Christmas Day my mother died following a battle with cancer.

Never in my life has it been so hard to get ready for the holiday season. Friends tell me that the first of everything is always the hardest and that time will ease some of the pain.

Her birthday is today, Dec. 20. She would have been 81.

Experiencing grief at what is for most people the most joyous time of year puts the holidays in a new light for me.

What I have seen is that the celebrations we enjoy each year together stay with us the rest of our lives. The memories we make when we are children last a lifetime.

And the story of the baby Jesus and that very first Christmas is the hope that lights our way through these dark times in our lives.

I think of how my mother worked so hard to make us a family, to build traditions that remind us of Christmas past.

My early Christmas memories are shaded in the black and white of a Kodak brownie camera. Like the images on those early televisions with screens that resembled half a gold fish bowl, the pictures in my mind are fuzzy and convoluted, almost too small to examine intricately.

Mother was always at the center, the heart of Christmas, decorating, cooking, shopping, wrapping, just like mothers always are.

Over the years we developed our Christmas scenario. On Christmas Eve we always gathered around in the living room to hang our stockings and read "The Night Before Christmas". I still have my Little Golden Book with my name written in my 6-year-old handwriting on the inside cover.

Our stockings were red felt with our names in gold glitter. Each of us would hang our own stockings one by one along the mantle in the living room.

Our decorations were simple, but the centerpiece was a manger scene with a little stable and figures. Each year setting that up was a special event at our house.

On Christmas we would always read out loud the story of the birth of Jesus in the Bible in the chapter of Luke just before we sat down to our Christmas dinner.

Our Christmas dinner was always the exact same menu, and we all always said that the dressing was the best it had ever been. My mother expected to hear those words just as much as we expected to find presents under the tree with our names on them.

Those Christmases of the 1960s as I got a little older are in Technicolor, almost too brightly hued, with matching plaid pajamas and little granny hats and big fluffy bedroom shoes. The first Barbies, Monopoly games, and Easy Bake Ovens for the girls, Hot Wheels sets for my brother.

But what I remember most is all of us together as a family. The gifts, the lights, the decorations, the smells and the sounds of Christmas were just the tinsel, the trappings to make everything merry and bright.

What gave it heart were the simple hugs and kind words, the peace that came when everything from the outside world was silent for just a little while, and our total focus centered on our family and our time together.

I will never spend another Christmas on this earth with my mother. I will never see her light up when I hand her some chocolate kisses that she always called silver bells and were her favorite candy. I will not see again the joy she got from receiving a pretty red poinsettia to place in the living room in a spot of honor, and I will never taste her wonderful cornbread dressing.

But what she gave me was the gift of herself, and what she taught me was how to give in return to my own family.

I hope each of you finds that quiet, still moment this Christmas that for me represents the true Christmas spirit.

Like the soft glow of a candle with a little paper around it held in the hand of a small child at a Christmas Eve service, the memories of all our special holidays with all those who mean and have meant so much to us brightens this holiday.

Merry Christmas to each of you.

Night Before Christmas Holds Special Meaning

Christmas Eve has always been my favorite day of the holiday time.

On Christmas Eve I love the late afternoon and early evening, as dusk falls as softly as snow, coloring the landscape in gentle grays, blues and roses, the colors of Mary and Joseph.

As night comes on, the lights within begin to shine a little brighter; the warmth permeates us as we begin to celebrate the most precious minutes and hours of the year.

If I sit quietly and gaze at the tree sparkling with its hundred twinkly lights, I can see Christmases past. On this one night, like no other, I feel my growing up family close at hand.

As I listen to the soft strains of carols in my memory I see my brother and sister and me sitting in the living room floor around our tree. I see my father peeling a tangerine and my mother setting the dining room table for Christmas morning breakfast.

The tree in my memory is a tall evergreen decked out with big colored lights and covered with a thousand little strands of icicles, red and green and gold balls and little paper bells. In the branches, my mother always nestled mine and my sister's little dolls.

We never had that many presents under the tree, but it was always enough. Exotically wrapped packages from my Aunt Elizabeth in Birmingham and my Uncle Grady in Newnan,

Rebecca Johnston

small carefully wrapped gifts from my grandmother nestled under the tree. A present for each of us, usually pajamas or slippers, from my mother.

Toys from Santa would appear the next morning.

But when I look back in my memory to those Christmases past, it isn't about the presents that I received. It is about all of us being together, the love we shared as a family.

Sitting together as a family while we read the Christmas story from the Bible, holding hands around the table while my father shared the blessing.

My mother gave us traditions and knit us together as a family and my father infused the whole thing with his special joy, his laughter, his sparkle. Those are the gifts that I remember.

Fast forward 20 years to the first real Christmas for me in my own home. It is Christmas Eve 1979 and I walk through the door of the first home Harry and I owned with a small bundle in my arms. Five days earlier, I had given birth to our first child.

Because of complications I stayed in the hospital for several days, and we weren't sure if I would get to come home for Christmas. But on Christmas Eve, my doctor made his rounds and told me that I could go home for the holiday.

I don't remember what we ate or whether we even had presents. What I do remember is all being together in our little house, the new arrival the center of all our attention, the joy and happiness that a new baby brings.

My parents came over to help with the baby and the meals and the clothes, the diapers and the bottles and all the work that goes with a brand new infant.

That night we sat together around our little tree and began the time of carrying on traditions that became with time our own.

As the years flew by we found the special peace and closeness growing stronger each year that being together brings. Christmas is the time that cements families together.

There was always the frantic shopping, cooking, and decorating that leads up to Christmas. But each year on Christmas Eve, if for only a few minutes, I would sit quietly and reflect on all that Christmas truly means.

Christmas Eve three years ago, my sister and brother, and our families gathered around my mother as she lay dying. We had prayed for her to get better, to rally and have some more time to spend with her family whom she loved so dearly. But it was just not to be.

As dusk fell on Christmas Eve she fell into a coma and by the next afternoon she went to be with Jesus. On the day that she always worked so hard to make special for us, God made special for her.

Now as I reflect this Christmas Eve I feel my mother close at hand, reminding me of all that Christmas really means. Hope, peace and joy. The promise of eternal life.

If I sit very quietly for even a moment on this Christmas Eve, my mind opens a window and I go back to all the times that mean so much to me and I thank God for sending us his Son.

And I know in my heart that it is Christmas.

Letter Communicates Meaning of Christmas

Dear Young People,

Christmas is hard to find and harder still to keep. I want to challenge each of you this year as you celebrate with your family to give your children the special gift of love and warmth and tradition that my parents gave me.

When I look back to my childhood, I remember vividly the little family traditions that we built year by year. Right after Thanksgiving we would ride to town, all five of us piled in the old Ford. We would keep our eyes peeled to see who could see the Christmas lights first. They would be strung, red and green, across Main Street, and my father would always say with excitement, "I'm going to see them first!" Then he would let one of us children be the one to shout out, "I see them, I see them."

The first decoration we would unpack and set up was the little manger scene and its little wooden stable. We would put it out on the table in the living room, unpacking each little figurine, then fluff some angel hair or greenery around it, giving it a place of honor in our holiday to mark the true meaning of Christmas.

Decorating the tree was a family affair. The tree would go up in the living room one week before Christmas Day. We always had a fresh green fir, cut down ourselves or purchased at a local tree lot. No artificial for us, no modern shiny aluminum tree or other attempt at a permanent decoration.

The smell of Christmas filled the house as we covered it in colored lights, shiny balls and those icicles made of plastic. My father would always say that it took it all to make it the perfect tree.

On Christmas Eve we would gather in the living room, the five of us, to read the Christmas story and hang our stockings. To this day I love Christmas Eve much more than Christmas Day. The anticipation, the feeling of peace and love that comes over us on that one special night of the year is to me the most magical time. We would take out the family Bible and, once I was old enough to read, I would help my father tell the beautiful story in Luke, Chapter 2.

Everyone had their special seat around the fireplace, the same place they would look for their gifts on Christmas morning. After reading the story of Jesus' birth, we would get out the old, tattered copy of "The Night Before Christmas" and take turns reading passages around the room. Most of us knew it by heart. Then we would hang up our stockings on the mantle, knowing that in the morning we would find an apple, an orange, and some candy in there.

Even when we no longer believed in Santa, my mother would not let us admit it. She always said that my younger brother still believed and that we had to keep him from finding out. We all knew that he had long ago figured things out, but we entered the conspiracy to believe. And so, we would go to sleep on Christmas Eve to wake up to presents, and food, and laughter and fun. We always opened our presents one by one to make it all last longer and to enjoy that special time.

The presents that I received have long been gone and forgotten, but those traditions live on. I brought many of them to my own family, adding others of our own. I hope that my children, who are grown now, will look back on their childhoods with the same joy I do. When I close my eyes, I can still feel the happiness and peace of my childhood Christmases, and remember the love my parents gave me through their time and their attention.

Today's world is so busy, hectic and fast-paced. We are bombarded with data and information, working hard to give our families the things they want, bigger televisions, faster computers, fancier cell phones. But I promise you that the greatest gift you can give your children is the gift of you. And the most precious memories are those of doing simple things like baking cookies or picking a Christmas tree or reading the Christmas story together.

Silent night, holy night, all is calm, all is bright. May the peace and joy of Christmas fill your heart and your family this holiday and may it carry you into the New Year.

Have a Happy Christmas,
Your Friend Rebecca

Giving to Others Wraps Up Shopping

Everywhere we go these days the question of the moment seems to be, have you finished your shopping yet?

Of course each of us has his or her own routine. Some people like to shop all year long storing up surprises like nuts for the winter, some like to wait until Christmas Eve and consider it a badge of courage to be the last shopper to hurry home from the malls.

My own brand of holiday shopping mania is to try to cram it all in between Thanksgiving and Christmas, and just like the overeating part of the season, I somehow don't feel like I am totally into the spirit of things until I have overspent.

And no matter how much I buy or that my "children" are now all grown up, on Christmas Eve when I pull everything out from all my little hiding places, it never looks like quite enough.

Growing up here in Canton, holiday shopping meant heading downtown with the money I had saved up from my allowance and doing some extra chores around the house. Sometimes my father would slip me an extra $10 bill to make sure I had plenty of funding for gifts. If I had $15, I would feel flush indeed.

I loved all the old stores in downtown Canton, from the dark and dignified McClure Book Store to Key's Jewelry Store to Canton Drug Co. on the corner.

Rebecca Johnston

Just like today when I go shopping and have trouble limiting my purchases for my favorite person on my list, me of course, I would love to window shop for things I wanted. The latest Nancy Drew mystery book, a new board game from the bookstore, a special sterling silver charm for my charm bracelet from those in the glass case at Key's, or the latest 45 record from Kessler's Five and Dime usually topped my list.

The real thrill of window shopping, though, came at Jones Mercantile Co. There the windows were all decked out for the holidays with a waving Santa, a legion of little elves, perhaps a few bears enjoying tea. When each holiday rolled around the long row of glass windows would look like Fifth Avenue to my young eyes.

From an early age, we were allowed to wander around the area, in and out of stores, choosing those gifts for everyone on our list. My beloved grandmother adored gloves and brightly colored handkerchiefs, baubles and beads of all kinds, pretty pins and earrings, clip-on of course.

My mother was a little harder to please. Finding the right gift for her took some real head scratching. The best way to make a hit with her seemed to be a pretty greeting card and something I made myself at school.

My father was easy to buy for, and always raved about any tie or tie tack, pair of socks or gloves or scarf I might choose.

Mostly, though, shopping in downtown Canton was a lot more about relationships than about merchandise. Everywhere you went, you knew everybody by name. The people who worked in the stores all knew me and my family, and everybody else's family too.

Canton was a lovely small town in those days. Everyone took pride in our community and cared about one another. This is not some Utopian dream that I made up, that was how it really was. At no time of year did that feeling of neighborliness and friendliness shine more than at Christmas.

Nowadays we spend a lot more time, effort and money on Christmas, and I think that what we are really trying to buy is that wonderful feeling we used to get so much more readily when life was simpler.

Christmas cards handwritten and addressed were eagerly awaited, opened and displayed. Little neighbor gifts meant so much to the recipient, but they meant a lot to the giver too.

I loved those Saturdays before Christmas when I would put my allowance money in my pocket and go to town to spend it on the ones I cared about. The shopping was as much fun as the rest of the holiday.

Our lives are so busy now, spent in the car driving here, there and everywhere, on the computer, listening to our headsets, tuning out the voices of our neighbors and our families.

It's nice at Christmas to just slow down a little and remember, not just the true meaning of Christmas which should of course be at the heart of our celebration, but also our family, friends and neighbors.

When I think back to my growing up days, I remember the fellowship and time together a lot more than the presents under the tree. Taking time to be nice to each other is often the best gift we can give or receive.

My holiday greeting for each of you is to hope you can slow down and savor Christmas Present while remembering the joys of Christmas Past.

Finding the Peace of Christmas

My Christmas wish is for peace, joy and hope this holiday.

For each of us I wish a holiday season filled with family, friends and loved ones. I hope for a time of celebration of that which is meaningful in our lives. I pray that we can look beyond the tinsel and hype and find the special magic that gives the true meaning to this time of year.

For those of us who are spending Christmas alone, or facing sickness in our families or other hardships, my Christmas wish is for some special miracle, big or small to make the heart lighter.

And if all else fails, we can each close our eyes, say a quiet prayer in our hearts and feel the peace of Jesus Christ steal over us.

Cherokee County is a community in flux. Constant change, growth, new neighbors moving in, old neighbors moving on. Those are the ebbs and flows of the tides around us. Change can be hard at any time of year, but especially at the holidays.

Many of us have left families far away and won't get to see their faces this holiday season. Many will be celebrating Christmas in a new house, a new community, and a new place, amid new traditions that seem strange and out of tune with what we imagine the holidays to be.

Many of our new neighbors will wish for snow on Christmas, the cold crisp weather that heralds the season in song, card and story.

Here in Cherokee County we generally have a softer kind of holiday weather, a Southern Christmas where the wind whispers through the pines and the sun comes out to warm the cool earth and remind us of the hope of spring just when we celebrate the darkest days of the year.

Christmas is mellower and kinder here, like an aged fruitcake soaked in spirits and swathed in cheesecloth.

I wish that this holiday season all of us can make our ways away from the malls, the rush of traffic, and the weariness of day-to-day life, and travel in our minds to the simpler times, the times of Christmas excitement and enjoyment by a child of baking cookies, or finding a stocking with candy and fruit spilling out.

Maybe reality is working at your job right up until Christmas, rushing to the grocery store at the last minute, and working your fingers to the bone to complete all the greeting cards and package wrapping, all the efforts to have that story book holiday.

But maybe, just maybe that storybook holiday isn't in expensive gifts, or perfectly decorated trees. Maybe it is already in our hearts, if we just look there instead.

My hope is that each of us finds the thing we are looking for the most this coming year. And that we know it when we find it and it has real meaning, not just the ephemeral trappings that so many of us run after.

My hope is that the story that unfolded two thousand years ago halfway around the world in a small town with an ordinary family in a simple stable will bring each of us the hope and peace and joy that is Christmas.

County Celebrates Christmas Birthday

In the middle of the holidays I always think about another birthday – the official date that Cherokee County was formed.

History books tell us that on Dec. 26, 1831, a law was enacted in Georgia creating Cherokee County. Our county was much, much larger then, 6,900 square miles to be exact. Today it is a mere 429 square miles, but still one of the larger counties in our area.

Everything that made up the original Cherokee County was theoretically owned by the Cherokee Indians. All remaining Indian Territory in the state was lumped into one large county and with one stroke of a pen declared to be a new county.

Many white settlers already occupied land in the new Cherokee County back in 1831. Many of them believed themselves by all rights to be the legal owners. But the federal government had continued to assure the Cherokee nation they owned the territory.

The new county included all land in northwest Georgia, from the Tennessee/North Carolina border down to the Carroll County line and everything west of the Chattahoochee River.

The land fight over Cherokee County was ugly. The federal government turned around and gave the land to Georgia in return for cooperation on Indian matters, the Cherokee Indians refused to settle on a price to be paid for the lands, and things turned bad.

Those were the days when Cherokee County was the frontier, the rough and tumble world where pioneers were pushing in to find homes and land for their families. They were called times of intensity, of blood, sweat and tears.

Right around the time of the founding of Cherokee County another event rocked north Georgia. Gold was found in "them thar hills."

The first gold rush of the nation started in north Georgia in 1830 when gold was found on a creek near Dahlonega. Within weeks more than 3,000 white men had pushed into the territory to search for gold.

It could be argued that the discovery of gold sealed the fate of the Cherokee nation.

Once the glitter of gold was shining in the eyes of the white men, they could easily be blinded to what was right or wrong. Not much different from today.

In 1832 the gold lottery began and Cherokee County was carved into several counties, a process that continued for the next 20 years as little by little about 20 counties were formed from the original territory.

In 1832 the county held its first elections and the first court of the county sat and worked to bring order to a chaotic world.

The first jury that was called in Cherokee County included the following men: James Hemphill, John Dawson, James Cantril, Franklin Daniel, Green Durham, Robert Fowler, John Jack, Reuben Sams, John P. Brooke, Charles Haynes, George Barber, Noble Timmons, John Holcomb, Leroy Hammond, Samuel Means, William Ray, Hubbard Baskin, Will Smith and William Lay.

Many of those names continue with descendants today.

Frank Daniel is one of the earliest white settlers to come to Cherokee County. The Holcombs, Timmonses and Eppersons were also among the earliest settlers in the county. John Epperson is said to have had no white neighbors and have traded with the Indians at a post he established as early as 1815.

Cherokee County had a turbulent first few years, fraught with controversy as the native inhabitants were forced away and land was grabbed by those pouring in.

Despite some pockets of gold, the region was poor and finding a living out of the hills and clay was hard.

Those were tough days peopled by tough men and women who were our forefathers.

Special Delivery Brightens Holiday

Christmas brings special memories of a lifetime to each of us. It is a time of reflection, of celebration, of togetherness. Christmas brings out the best in us, in mankind as a whole. For one day we celebrate peace on earth, good will to men.

Christmas touches the child in all of us. We are allowed to tear away the shell of daily life and for a brief moment each year just enjoy with heartfelt abandon the tastes and sounds and smells of the season. Perhaps we are a little excessive, a little extravagant, but that's all right.

I hope each of us has the opportunity to give one act of kindness to someone this holiday season. It could be allowing someone in front of us in line, or a visit to a neighbor we haven't seen in a while, or a call to a relative we haven't heard from recently. It could be sharing something with someone who is having a tough time this holiday, or taking time to comfort someone who has suffered a loss this year.

I hope too that we can make one resolution for the New Year to remember the feeling Christmas brings and to find a way sometime this year to do something that keeps alive that spirit of love and kindness.

I remember each year at this time the birth of my only son. My husband and I went to the hospital on Dec. 17, 1979. Thirty-six hours later on Dec. 19 at 2 A.M. Nathan Harvey Johnston was born.

Being in the hospital right before Christmas can be a time of good cheer and on the maternity ward it was just that. Everywhere you turned Christmas decorations were gaily hung, bright dashes of seasonal flowers could be seen scattered about, and everyone with a new baby had something most special and wonderful to celebrate.

But a hospital can be a tough time during the holidays if you are there for a less fortunate reason, and of course most people are. Ambulances come in late at night. Elderly patients often have few if any visitors. Children who are sick break your heart that they are in such a place instead of at home enjoying all the best of the holiday.

Although my holiday visit was for a joyous reason, I had a rough time and some minor complications. But no matter how I felt, I so badly wanted to be home for Christmas. On Christmas Eve morning, the doctor came in to check me out and give me the good news. We could go home.

And home never looked so good. That was one of the best Christmases of my life and it started a lifetime as a new family. I also discovered what it means to love a child. That is a special emotion.

I think about God deciding to sacrifice his Son for us and my gratitude is boundless.

A writer once wrote the following about the life of Christ and I wanted to share it with you this holiday season.

"He was born in a stable, in an obscure village, the child of a peasant woman. He worked in a carpenter's shop until he was 30. From there he traveled less than 200 miles. He never wrote a book. He never held office. He never had a family or owned a home. He did none of the things one associates with greatness. He became a nomadic preacher. He was only 33 when the tide of popular opinion turned against him. He was betrayed by a close friend, and his other friends ran away. He was turned over to his enemies and went through the mockery of a trial. He was unjustly condemned to death, crucified on a cross between two thieves, on a hill overlooking the town dump. And when dead, was laid in a borrowed grave, through the pity of a friend. Nineteen centuries have come and gone, and all the armies that ever marched, all the navies that ever sailed, all the parliaments that ever sat, and all the kings that ever reigned have not affected the life of man on this earth as that One Solitary Life. He is the central figure of the human race; He is the Messiah, the Son of God, Jesus Christ."

Santa Tim is A Jolly Old Elf

When we think Santa Claus in Cherokee County Tim Cavender always comes to mind.

I am one of those people who still believes, who still hears the bells of Christmas and knows that there is a real Santa Claus, and so in my mind Tim is Santa's jolliest elf here in the real world.

Tim has built up quite a reputation as the Santa who hands out a few switches and lumps of coal in the form of some barbed comments about our elected officials and leaders each year at the annual Cherokee County Chamber of Commerce Christmas breakfast.

But there is a kinder, gentler Santa Tim.

For 30 years Tim has been visiting Cherokee County folks of all ages, spreading good cheer. He visits nursing homes in his Santa uniform, delighting the elderly residents.

Santa Tim has long traveled the byways and highways of Cherokee visiting little boys and girls and assuring them that Santa has them on his list. Santa Tim spreads magic wherever he goes.

When my children were little, Santa Tim would make a surprise visit to the Kiwanis Club Christmas party at the Canton Golf Club each year. Santa's helper Ray DeLuca and the other

Kiwanis dads would make sure that there was a wrapped gift for each of the children in attendance.

The children would crowd around him or sit on his lap and look at him with awe as he spoke in that deep baritone we know is what the real Santa sounds like.

Of course there were always the skeptics, the children who looked closely to see if his beard was real, who would comment that he drove up in a car, not in a sleigh pulled by reindeer.

But somehow Tim always quieted the critics and helped us keep the faith.

Last week Santa Tim spoke to the Rotary Club of Canton, and he shared some of his fond memories of Christmas in Cherokee County when he was growing up as a small boy in Ball Ground.

He told of riding into Canton to see the tinsel and lights. He told of strolling through the old stores, Kessler's toy land and others, and the delight that he would feel at surveying the riches therein.

He reminded us of the days when Santa would arrive in a helicopter that landed in the parking lot of Jones Mercantile Store, the site of today's Cherokee County Justice Center. He told about the throngs of children who would be screaming and cheering at the opportunity to see Santa arrive.

He talked about the little house in the Canton square where Santa sat all the days leading up to Christmas and where youngsters could go to speak to old St. Nick and whisper their most secret wishes.

He reminded us of the days when the commercial aspects of Christmas were less emphasized, and the real meaning of Christmas, the birth of Jesus, given a greater part in the pageantry of the season.

Finally he wove around us a beautiful story of a man who longed for Jesus to visit at his house, and how his wishes were realized, but in a way that was different from what he expected.

For just a few minutes he helped us pause and remember in our hearts what each of us really wants from the Christmas season, and where to look beneath the tinsel and the glitter and the gifts to find it.

Santa Tim helps little children and old folks and even busy adults who often spend too much time caught up in their own careers and pursuits to find the spirit of Christmas.

Thanks, Santa Tim, for helping us to believe.

Lights of Christmas Sparkle Brightly

Christmas is a time of shadow, of light, and of dreams.

In the shadows of our minds they wait, the memories of our Christmases past. The loved ones who are no longer here, the vignettes of other times, other places, other celebrations.

We remember the times when our parents held us close, wrapped in the safe secure blanket of love.

As we gaze into the flickering fire of the Yule season we see the faces of our grandparents, smiling at us. We see our brothers and sisters as little children, sitting under the holiday trees of our childhoods.

We recall family feasts, and gatherings of relatives from near and far. Aunts and uncles and cousins all stand sentinel in the shadows of our memory, taking us back into the safe haven of childhood, of days of innocence when we believed in all that is good and kind and pure.

Our minds touch briefly on the tinsel and the glitter and the trimmings of the season, the gifts and frivolity, the giving and receiving. We recall the laughter and the song and the celebration.

Then from the dim recesses comes the warmth of peace that symbolizes the real meaning of the season.

Our memories of all the years before gather round us, drawing closer and closer until our hearts are warmed and filled with love. Those are the memories of our Christmases past.

Then out of the shadows we move into the light of Christmas present.

We see the sparkle and twinkle of a million small white lights reflected in the glowing eyes of our children. We feel their little arms reach up to us and encircle us with the confidence of a new generation.

We open our doors and let the light of holiday friendship spill out into the darkness of the winter night, and the glow of the season lights the path to us.

We reach out our hands and our hearts to our friends and family in the bright light of Christmas present and we feel the camaraderie of the season.

We look around as we gather in church for the candlelight service, and we see the light of Christmas glowing brightly this holiday.

Our hearts swell with hope and lightness, our worries are lifted, and we see with clear eyes the good in our fellow man and in ourselves. That is the light of Christmas present.

We close our eyes and let the dreams of Christmas future come in, the dreams of how things should be and will be.

Like gentle clouds of soft white, like moonlight on a stark landscape, like fog and snow swirling around us, the mists of Christmas future beckon.

We know not what those Christmases future will bring, we only know that through continued dreams and beliefs in the intrinsic

Rebecca Johnston

goodness of our fellow man, in the promise of the Christ child we find the hope of days to come.

No matter how bleak some times seem, no matter how much pain and suffering there is in the world, no matter how cold and dark the night of winter, there is the promise of Christmas future.

And so we close our eyes and drift to sleep this Christmas with the promise of the future, the light of today and the memories of yesteryear to keep us warm and safe.

For one day, one moment in the time of our busy lives the joy, the peace, the love of Christmas shines brighter than any other light and we know that life is precious and good.

NEW YEAR'S DAY

Photo courtesy of Cherokee County Historical Society
A snow storm blankets Main Street in Canton in 1961.

> Ring out the old, ring in the new
> Ring, happy bells, across the snow:
> The year is going, let him go;
> Ring out the false, ring in the true.
>   Lord Tennyson

New Year's Trivia Proves Fun Pursuit

One of those fun New Year traditions for a group of our friends and family is to eat plenty of ham, turnip greens and black-eyed peas, watch a little football and then settle in for a game of Trivial Pursuit.

We play guys against the girls, and it can often get intense. We are a multi-generational group and that adds to the fun.

January 4 is National Trivia Day and in response to that momentous event, the makers of Trivial Pursuit, Hasbro Games, released its list of the most trivial events and people of the year 2003.

We have Joe Millionaire at Number 10, who was cheered on by at least a million fans, and Number Nine was David Blaine, who suspended himself above London in a box.

At Number Eight, there was the arrests of music swappers, including a little girl of 13, who was one of the first to pay her fines and settle her account.

Jessica Simpson rang in at Number Seven, and Brittney and Madonna and their little display at the Music Awards captured the Number Six spot of Trivial Events.

The Baseball Curses of the 2003 Season rang in at Number Five. The Hasbro folks said you couldn't have scripted it better – or worse, depending on whom you were cheering for – than the real story.

Queer Eye for the Straight Guy took the Number Four poll. That is the strangest phenomenon I have witnessed in our society in a long while.

The California Recall was Number Three. In years to come, when the game question is what man who played a crazed robot, groped women and spoke with a heavy accent made it to the top slot in California, I will know the answer. What I won't recall is whom he beat out to get there.

Number Two is Bennifer – need we say more?

And the Number One Trivial Moment of the Year is Paris Hilton.

Now this short list of the good, the bad and the ugly of the year got me thinking about Cherokee County.

Many folks are already playing the Cherokeeopoly Game, which could mirror real life in which developers try to buy up everything in sight and pile as many houses as possible on the smallest and cheapest spaces on the board.

But what about some trivia for Cherokee County?

Questions for the year of 2003 could go something like this.

What group of officials came down off their mount and finally united on an issue, voting to place the Ten Commandments in a government building? Although almost certain to face defeat on another game board, the Pursuit of Justice, they still decided to hang the document.

Which local city's officials went after women's professional soccer as a means of putting them on the map, only to have their plans booted out of the stadium with the demise of the women's soccer league?

Which group of officials researched how to take 180 days and divide them by 12 and come up with a plan that had some folks packing their bags and others scratching their heads?

How many losing seasons did the hometown favorite football team endure before going to the state semi-finals?

Which PGA player made Woodstock, Georgia, the most important Woodstock and had more people volunteering to man concession stands than ever in the history of the county?

Which city in Cherokee County had more people running for election in 2003 than had ever actually voted in a city election in years past?

Which developer and former commission chair candidate tried to turn Freedom Ranch into Taxpayer's Farm?

Which small north Cherokee town has a new motto about its rocks?

Which local dairy had an amazing year?

If you know the answers to most of those trivial questions about our community, you can roll the dice and head into the New Year.

Whatever is ahead, it is sure to be fun. Happy New Year.

Resolution to Care About Community

The New Year always brings new resolutions and a look ahead to the clean slate before us.

Cherokee County has a great opportunity to write our future, to make our community all that it should and could be. When our forefathers wrote the charter and incorporated this county in the bleak winter of 1833, they started us on a journey that has never faltered in growth, prosperity and improvements for the residents who live here.

Our local history relays a story of continuous achievement and improvement. We were a farming community, but one that grew hefty bank accounts and solid legacies for the families who farmed. Dairy farming, feed and farm equipment, cotton, and poultry were all thriving parts of our local economy.

We were a mining town, one where the abundant natural resources, marble, copper and even gold, were taken from the ground and given new life. Marble from our hills was sent far and wide for use in monuments and buildings.

We were a mill town, one that took pride in that distinction. Our mill village had streets that were tree lined and paved. Houses were neat and well-maintained, and a school and other facilities were built to enhance the neighborhood.

The denim we produced was held in high respect nationwide, and wherever you lived, there is a chance your grandfather's work pants and overalls were made with Canton cloth.

Our educational system always enjoyed a high reputation. Canton High School was considered a porthole to higher learning, and each school, large or small, took pride in what the students there were able to learn.

Our banks were sound, even in time of hardship. People paid their bills, saved their wages, and practiced conservative spending habits.

Residents attended church regularly and faithfully. Church life was at the heart of the community, and members of the community lived what they learned.

All in all, the people of Cherokee County built a legacy of good moral principles, hard work, care for one another and those less fortunate and pride in community. Read any of the histories of this community and the story unfolds of a special place.

We've grown, we've changed, and many newcomers have made this their home in the ensuing decades since our county was born. But the heart of the community remains. Residents take pride in what we have and want to enhance it rather than destroy it. They love the rural beauty, the boundless natural resources. No matter what route you take to come home to Cherokee County, the serenity seems to engulf you and you leave behind the hurly-burly of the city.

I would like to see us all join together and make it our New Year's resolution to do at least one thing this year to improve our community. There are many ways big and small that we can make a difference.

Get involved at our children's school or in our church.

Rebecca Johnston

Stop and pick up litter along a county road. Never litter ourselves.

Recycle, so that our landfills can last a little longer.

Save money and buy locally, so that our local economy remains strong.

Contribute to a civic organization, help a neighbor.

Make sure to vote. Keep informed on the issues that affect our daily lives.

Plant a tree.

Walk somewhere instead of driving.

Simple contributions like those and others you may think of can help our community live up to our legacy.

We are firmly launched on the road to a new century and a new millennium. But we in Cherokee County have a history that we can trace with pride, and a chance to leave those that come after us the kind of place we found when we came this way.

Valentine's Day

Frances and Ralph Owen celebrate their anniversary.

"Life's greatest happiness is to be convinced we are loved."
                              Victor Hugo

Ralph and Frances Owen Were True Loves

A special Valentine couple that always comes to mind when I think of true love and fine folks is Ralph and Frances Owen. Although now in their 90s, they still exemplify commitment and dedication to a relationship and to each other.

I have interviewed them several times over my career and use their individual writings to research many historical elements of our community. They are role models to me and I am sure to many others in this community, and their contributions are legion. Growing up, the arrival of the local newspaper was a highlight of the week in Canton. Mr. Owen and his brother were the editors and publishers of the North Georgia Tribune, now the Cherokee Tribune, for more than 30 years. They chronicled the daily life of our community, and told us of the major events and local reaction for much of the heart of the past century. Their columns and musings kept us amused, interested, provoked and always talking.

Ralph Owen gave back to the community as editor. He was involved on every level during his career. Getting the newspaper to press and on the streets is a responsibility and duty, as well as a joy for people in the newspaper business.

One of my favorite stories from Mr. Owen tells of the trials that sometimes make it hard. In June of 1955, fire swept through the newspaper office, and through portions of downtown Canton.

Rebecca Johnston

The building that housed the Tribune was mostly destroyed. But the paper did not miss an issue, and was printed in Dalton for the four months it took to rebuild the facilities in Canton. The fire started in Cantex, a manufacturing plant in the downtown area. A picture of the sewing room of that facility hangs in the Tribune office today.

The plant was housed in the four-story Coggins-Jones building. According to published accounts, a hot wind was blowing and the intense fire could not be brought under control until a whole block of downtown Canton burned.

Faced with a major story and nowhere local to print, resourcefulness was necessary. True grit was needed and the situation was grim, but the paper went out. That type of work ethic and perseverance is what makes a person strong. Sometimes it seems as if the newer philosophy is that if things don't come easy, why bother? But people like Ralph Owen stand as a reminder of how we ought to handle our business and our personal lives.

I think my memory serves me right when I say that Mr. Owen came to town from Pickens County, where he was affiliated with the newspaper that took over ownership of the Tribune in 1944. His wife, Frances Rudasill Owen, was no stranger to the news. Her father was at one time publisher and editor of the Cherokee Advance.

This couple's love of the written word, of the history of Cherokee County and of family and each other is a true inspiration to me. Mrs. Owen has written on such diverse topics as moonshine and local history. She is a proponent of the importance of reading and public libraries, of things cultural and things real. I just hope that when I look back on my life, I can have made one one-100th the difference in this community that Ralph and Frances Owen have made.

The dedication of people like them is what has forged Cherokee County into a special place to live. A marriage that has spanned decades, a dedication to the place they live and to their neighbors, a fine religious belief, a love of gardening and all things lovely. What a delightful Valentine couple.

Always Let Man Have Last Word

My grandmother taught me a lot about love. I don't mean the grandmother-granddaughter kind, either. I mean the kind of love between a man and a woman that lasts a lifetime and even longer.

I doubt my dear Gran received many Valentine cards or hearts and candy from her husband, but the two had a strong love that survived World War I, the Great Depression and even death.

My grandfather died of a heart attack when he was just 55 years old. He went to work at the Marble Plant near the Etowah River one sunny morning feeling just fine, and died only a few hours later.

My grandmother was 50 at the time and she lived for 48 more years, another whole lifetime, but she never quit loving her Henry.

While her devotion and tenderness toward my grandfather was a lesson in itself, it was her gentle way of reminding me how to behave that influences me even today.

One piece of advice she always gave me was to never go to bed angry at each other.

Another that is more difficult to follow for me, and will have the feminists up in arms, was always let the man have the last word.

Her most important mantra was that the way to a man's heart is through his stomach. Southern cooking - perfectly fried chicken, creamy, dreamy macaroni and cheese, melt-in-your-mouth biscuits and delicate pound cake - was designed to please the male palate.

Any wife who did not greet her husband in the morning with a hot, tasty breakfast on the table and welcome him home in the evening with a home-cooked dinner was just plain slovenly.

Perhaps her biggest influence in my life was that she picked out my husband for me, and then she used all her considerable skills to make sure that I picked him and he chose me too.

From the moment she saw my future Mister walk into the First Baptist Church of Canton for the annual Lottie Moon Christmas program, she knew what she wanted. He was so mannerly, so Christian, such a nice young man. That he was only 12 at the time - and so was I - did not deter her.

It would be 12 more years before we would marry, but basically the deal was sealed, the marriage contract struck when we were in the sixth grade.

By the time we were 16 she was allowing me to have him to dinner at her house once a week.

My mother didn't like a lot of courting during the week and she frowned on having a boy over on a school night. But Gran was just fine with it, as long as it was Harry.

After dinner we would sit in her front parlor and "get our homework" while she cleaned the kitchen and washed the dishes by hand.

When we both went away to college, a chapter of our lives was over. We both met new people, dated others.

But trust me; my grandmother never liked any of my choices. She didn't really say anything. She would just sort of purse her lips and her eyes would look away at the mention of any new boyfriend.

College ended and somehow, Harry and I got back together. I am sure my grandmother had some hand in it.

When we told her we were engaged she was ecstatic, and the day we got married was one of the pinnacles of her life.

It was a heart-stopping moment for me, too. Thirty-two years later I know that my grandmother in all her wisdom helped me make the right decision.

In her gentle way that never entailed a harsh word or a raised voice, she directed me to a sound love and marriage that has lasted through the years.

She tried her best, too, to make me a good wife. Most of her advice is hard for me to follow. But I know that she was always right.

It's just so difficult to let the man always have the last word.

Valentine's Day Recalls Exceptional Teacher

The first time I saw Jackie Jones Hopkins I thought she was so beautiful. She was like some exotic flower that had sprung up in our midst.

I was 10 years old and it was the first day of school of my fifth-grade year at Canton Elementary. Miss Jones, as she was then, was my new teacher. She looked like Jackie Kennedy, or the brunette bubble-cut Barbie doll.

These were the early days of Camelot, when the entire world had its eyes on a dazzling young couple who had waltzed into the White House. When everything was still fresh and innocent and new.

You must remember that Canton Elementary was a place of old things: old wooden floors soaked in oils from a million years of sweeping, old books from before the wars and a bevy of old-maid teachers. They were wonderful teachers, ladies like the Bozeman and Johnston sisters, who wore durable long wool skirts and brougham shoes, teachers who remembered my daddy when he was a boy and roamed those same halls of Old Canton Elementary on Academy Street.

And of course there was our principal, Shault Coker, who looked to me like an elderly Ichabod Crane worn down from a lifetime of keeping after lazy, irreverent students. Someone you wanted to make sure you never got in trouble with.

The first day of school was always one of excitement, wondering which teacher you got and who was in your class. When I walked up the wide steps, down the long hall, and into the second-story classroom in the big building, I entered a year that would bring a lot of change to our lives.

Miss Jones dressed in bouffant pastel dresses. She smiled and listened and planned a hundred exciting projects that would lead us on a path of adventure. She brought a touch of sophistication into our small town world.

Let me assure you that she was a tough teacher and discipline was never slack. One of the boys called her Fireball Jones and got in a world of trouble. Those were the days of the paddle, when teachers weren't afraid to apply a little capital punishment. But the girls in the class didn't need a lot of discipline. A promise to be the one to go with Miss Jones to clean the erasers by hitting them on a big stump in the schoolyard was enough to keep us in line.

Projects from that year still stand out in my mind. One was to fix an aquarium to display in the downstairs hall for all students to enjoy. We studied the different kinds of fish. I was especially fascinated by the habits of the piranha.

Miss Jones then drove us in her personal car all the way to Lenox Square, the only mall back then and the closest fish supply store, to purchase the fish and supplies. She took us in small groups of five students over a series of weeks until the aquarium was filled and complete.

But what always brings Miss Jones to mind is Valentine's Day. Right before Valentine's, my appendix almost ruptured. I was rushed to the brand new R.T. Jones Hospital and Dr. Grady Coker took it out. Instead of being with my friends, exchanging cards and candy, I was lying in the hospital for seven days to recuperate.

That's how we did things in those days before HMOs, we stayed in the hospital until we were practically well. I was fairly sad at missing Valentine's, but somehow Miss Jones must have known that.

She came to see me in the hospital and brought my little decorated shoebox filled with messages from my classmates. And she brought an orchid corsage and pinned it on my pillow. I thought that was the most beautiful, exotic thing in the world.

Maybe back in those days we didn't have a lot of education legislation or governmental plans or mandates. What we did have were caring teachers willing to go the extra mile.

I know there are still a lot of those out there. And if you ever wonder if you are appreciated, know that over the years and time and memories, I can still see Miss Jones clearly in my mind. I can still remember all the things we did my fifth-grade year.

It didn't surprise me that she led the way on technology in our school system, or that her contributions have opened new doors now for thousands and thousands of students.

I am just glad I was in her first class at her first teaching job in the little town of Canton.

Couples Keep Romance in Holiday

As any girl who came of age in the sixties would be, I was devastated to read the news that Barbie and Ken are breaking up after 43 years together.

That this news comes at Valentine's, the season when couples celebrate romance, dedication and commitment, is doubly sad.

I was fortunate enough to have one of the original Barbie's, sleekly dressed in a black and white strapless bathing suit to show her figure off to full advantage, white sunglasses in hand, her pierced ears, high heels and ponytail perfectly accessorizing.

It wasn't long before my perfect Barbie was joined by my perfect Ken, one of the originals also, with a strong physique, tall dark and handsome, sporting a crown of black hair and caring, sensual eyes.

One of my first gifts was the bride and groom attire, a lovely beaded white gown for Barbie, black tux for Ken. Soon, I had the apron for Barbie, the golf outfit for Ken, and an array of clothes for every career imaginable.

As the years passed, the wear and tear of daily life left my Ken and Barbie a little less perfect. Ken's hair got worn off in spots, Barbie's ponytail was less perky, but they were still together.

Now I am told that Barbie has a new tan and a new pocketbook and she is looking around. Bye-bye Ken, hello new adventures.

Fortunately, in real life this Valentine's Day, there are plenty of real couples around who continue to show that Cupid's arrow can last a lifetime, and that like fine wine, true love only improves with age. A lasting relationship can be tempered by the bad times and polished by the good times until it is as enduring and gleaming as steel.

When I think of great couples, one of the first to come to mind is Dr. William "Bill" Nichols and his lovely wife Martha. Their great and long marriage has spanned a number of decades. Their union has produced four wonderful daughters and a mental scrapbook of the most beautiful of memories.

Today, when I see them together, it is always evident how devoted they remain.

Another fabulous couple is Joyce and Harold Swindell. They just always seem to be having such great times together. The fun they share spills over onto all those around them.

They are always upbeat in a good way, getting the most out of everything they do, zipping through life holding hands and smiling all the way. They make being married look almost easy.

No mention of great couples would be complete without mentioning Miss Peggy and Mr. Louis Jones. What devotion, what caring and admiration and acceptance they have always had for each other.

Miss Peggy calls a lot of people "darling" in the old-fashioned way of the South, but when she says it to Mr. Louis, you know she means it in a deep and special way.

I look at our young couples today, and I see many who are embarking upon this wonderful, glorious journey of discovery, endurance, delight and perseverance. My message to them is that it isn't always easy, but it is worth it.

There are many seasons to love, and it can last a lifetime.

My advice to Barbie – give Ken another chance. If he shows up on your doorstep this Valentine's Day with a bouquet of roses, open your door and your heart wide. Forty-three years is too long to throw away on a whim.

You belong together. Happy Valentine's Day.

Valentine's Day No Time for War

This Valentine's Day has been one of dichotomies. Hearts and flowers make strange companions to fear of biological warfare.

During the traditional season of love it is sad to see our country rocked with fear of terrorists and issues of warnings, mounting tensions worldwide and escalating military preparations.

This victory can only be won by exercising mind over matter, by whistling a little tune, looking on the sunny side of life, practicing our faith and sending fear packing into the shadows where it belongs.

My great-grandmother Genervie Hughes Cochran lived to be 99 years old. She died just after World War II in 1946. In her lifetime she saw the Civil War, the two World Wars and a host of skirmishes.

Family accounts say she was 17 years old when General Sherman marched through Georgia. She lived with her parents on a farm somewhere between Canton and Waleska.

When word came that the Northern troops were near their home, my great-great-grandfather hid my grandmother and the other children in the loft of the barn in the hay. There they could get a view of what was happening through cracks in the wall of the barn.

Rebecca Johnston

Federal troops rode into the farmyard and demanded all the foodstuffs including hams and canned goods that the family had available.

The soldiers placed the foods in large pots in the yard and built up fires under them. But while the food was cooking the guard on the hill fired a shot that the Southern cavalry was approaching.

The Yankees saddled up and rode out, leaving the cook fires still going. The family could not salvage the food, which was a winter's worth of provisions for the isolated farm family.

That night the sky over Canton was lighted with a glare. The family watched in fear of what might be happening.

They later learned that the Northern troops burned the wooden bridge over the Etowah River leading into town and most of the buildings along Main Street.

Other local accounts tell of Sherman and his men foraging the area for supplies after fighting the battle of Resaca over to our west.

Many of the local men were fighting with Lee in Virginia at the time of the attack on our community, which happened in the spring of 1864. Those who were left were mostly older or very young. But a few men left in the hill country around Canton who had refused to sign up for the Cause fought a type of guerilla warfare against Sherman and his men, sending raiding parties to steal from the troops.

Many homes were spared by the Northern troops, some for displaying Masonic symbols, others where folks prevailed on the sympathies of the troops.

When I think about the recent outbreak of fear that our country will be attacked, when I see the panicked buying of supplies to reinforce our homes against a different, more sinister attack by foreigners this time, I think about those long-ago times.

I think about farmers wanting to protect their families, children scared, mothers worried. And I know that the same courage that ran through their veins, the same strength and grit that allowed them to survive will see us through these dark times as well.

The only way the terrorists can win is to make us afraid to go about our lives. By celebrating our freedom each day and by remembering our heritage we will persevere.

As we prepare for war, whether we agree with it or not, we must all commit ourselves to victory and to keeping the flame of freedom alive, just as our ancestors did.

Easter

Jim Jr., Rebecca and Carole Ann and mother Vern Wheeler celebrate Easter Sunday 1961.

"For I remember it is Easter morn, and life and love and peace are all new born."
      Alice Freeman Palmer

A First Baptist Easter Celebration

As a little girl nothing pleased me more than putting on my Easter bonnet, my frilly dress with umpteen petticoats and crinolines under it and my new shiny patent leather shoes with little pocketbook to match.

We didn't need an Easter parade in Canton; we had the First Baptist Church for that.

Everyone in town would don their new Sunday best and head to church on Easter morning. I was a member of a dedicated Baptist family, with a father who was a Deacon and a family motto of being there every time the doors were open.

But a lot of people showed up only on Easter Sunday, so it was always with interest and excitement that I set off to church on that holy holiday. Easter baskets of candy and eggs didn't hold half the attraction of a Sunday school class crammed with strange children and a brand new outfit to show off.

First Baptist would always be filled to overflowing, with chairs lining the aisles, and the partitions to the Sunday school rooms on either side of the sanctuary thrown open to provide additional seating. Regular Sundays were bleak compared to this one.

Even the Herald would be decked out in Easter finery for the occasion.

Rebecca Johnston

In the South a lot of our early understanding of religion came from the paper fans we used in church to provide some old-fashioned air conditioning.

When I think about my earliest thoughts of the significance of Easter, I see Jesus as he was depicted on those fans. When I think of Jesus praying in the Garden or riding triumphant into Jerusalem or the empty tomb, I see those wonderful watercolor pictures that adorned the pew fans.

In First Baptist Church Canton my grandmother had a special little pew next to the vestibule that was "her" seat in that church. She attended church there for something like 80 years. I think she joined it around the turn of the century, that's 1900, not 2000. And she always sat in that one place.

Gran as she was called by family and friends alike would sit on that little pew with back erect and hands delicately crossed. She had been a widow on a "fixed income" since 1935 when her husband died, and she made and designed all her own clothes. But her spring dresses were always elegant to me, light lawn or organdy pin-tucked and pleated in lovely pastel colors.

Her little weaknesses were orchids, and Easter was a time for a pretty corsage, pearls, white gloves and delicate handkerchiefs. I still have boxes and boxes of her gloves and handkerchiefs, many of them in colors to match a specific outfit, others trimmed with hand-worked lace or monograms.

She also had a lovely lavender shawl that she had crocheted and that was certainly one of her prides and joys.

She would cap off her outfit with a matching hat, in those days a pillbox to emulate the First Lady, trimmed with a little short veil. She wore her silver hair neatly pinned up into a French twist. She always powdered her nose and applied a light dusting of rouge and lipstick to complete her look.

I never saw her when she was not dressed with stockings, makeup, the entire deal, in all the years of her life that I shared. She lived alone until she was over 95 years of age, and was always as we said in my family "sharp as a tack."

On Easter she always wanted to get her seat early, in case some unknowing soul who didn't attend regularly tried to claim her pew. She also liked to have a good vantage point to check over all the other ladies and their outfits as they came in. Monday would be a day for discussing with all her friends what everyone had on. "I just can't imagine what she must have paid for that," "Wasn't that dress cut a little low?" "She always knows just the right thing to wear." "Didn't she look just lovely?"

Easter Sunday lunch might mean a trip to the Pine Crest Restaurant for the wonderful after church ritual that we always loved, or perhaps back home for Southern baked ham, potato salad and deviled eggs.

Then an afternoon of running around in the front yard hiding eggs, and eating more candy than we normally saw in two months.

Easter was a major event in those days, perhaps because our regular routine in a small town in rural north Georgia was pretty monotonous. But I am glad that I grew up when we had less, when our senses could be delighted with the smell of fresh mowed grass and the sight of the white dogwoods dazzling against the bright blue spring sky. When finding the prize egg was a major thrill and a new dress a stand-out occasion.

And when going to church on Easter morning in my Easter bonnet with all the frills upon it was the most important event of the season.

Hometown Holidays

Cissy and Paul Jones, here in a portrait used on a Christmas card, were neighbors with Rebecca and her family for more than 25 years and remain close friends today.

Gran and Rebecca loved to walk along Main Street. They always enjoyed a special relationship.

79

Rebecca Johnston

Jackie Jones Hopkins was Rebecca's fifth-grade teacher at Canton Elementary. It was Mrs. Hopkin's first year as a teacher.

Jeannie Lathem Adams is happy about what Santa brought. Her mother, Sara Lathem, always flocks a live tree with 'snow' and decorates it all in red, a favorite holiday memory of Rebecca's.

Hometown Holidays

This Christmas scene features Nancy Jones, along with brothers Frank Jones and Louis Jones, on the porch of the family home in downtown Canton, all decked out for the holidays.

Santa Tim, or Tim Cavender as he is known as the rest of year, hears from little Ann Johnston about what she wants for Christmas at the annual Kiwanis Christmas party at the Canton Golf Club.

Parades like this one through downtown Canton were annual events to kick off the holiday season. Usually held the weekend of Thanksgiving, merchants, schools, and organizations all got into the spirit.

Daria Allen, Nancy Jones and Rebecca, along with Mrs. Peggy Jones, are ready for trick or treating along Main Street. They are at the Halloween Carnival in the old Canton Elementary Gymnasium that stood behind the school on Academy Street.

New Clothes Dress Up Easter

Growing up, Easter meant a lot of different things to me. My family was deeply religious, especially my grandmother.

My grandmother lived a quiet life in her house on Main Street in Canton. Her days were spent listening to the religious programming on the radio, reading her Bible, and poring over Southern Baptist literature that she received in large quantities.

We all went to church every Sunday. In fact, I can truthfully say that in my youth, we went to church every time the doors were open, morning, noon and night.

But religion wasn't something reserved for church.

We fanned ourselves as we sat on my grandmother's porch with fans from the funeral homes and drug stores that depicted scenes in glorious Technicolor of all the important events in Jesus' life. We sang hymns, we memorized Bible versus, and we did all the normal activities of youth growing up in the heart of the Bible belt. Religion was an all-year-long kind of thing. Not just reserved for Easter

While Easter was a special religious time for us, what really set the holiday apart for me as a

Rebecca Johnston

child from normal church activities were all the other trappings.

Easter meant new clothes. And not just any new clothes. Elaborate outfits complete with hats garnished with bows and flowers and shiny white patent leather shoes. Fluffy dresses with rows of lace flowing gracefully over stiff white petticoats. And for my brother, little suits with short pants and bow ties.

I can still remember the smell of those new dresses made from organdy and dotted Swiss, purchased at Kiddie's Korner, THE children's shop in south Canton. Or more often, the booty from a shopping trip to Davison's in downtown Atlanta.

I loved those shopping trips to Atlanta with our whole family. Made only once or twice a year, my father would entertain us children while my mother took one child at a time to try on shiny new clothes. We might go to the Varsity for a chili dog and onion rings, or over to Piedmont Park to play in the early spring sunshine.

I especially loved shopping for shoes, a trend that has lasted a lifetime, as my closet would reveal.

Back then, you could try on a pair of shoes and slip your feet into an x-ray machine so that the sales person could accurately ascertain whether the shoes were an exact fit. That the machine might cause cancer only became apparent years later.

If you were really lucky and bought a certain brand of shoes, you were the proud recipient of a golden egg. Inside that egg was an array of goodies and treats.

But those treats were just a warm-up for the main attraction on Easter morning, the visit from the Easter Bunny!

I don't think my family was unusual in those days in that children did not receive presents and toys all the time. We spent a great deal of our time outside, riding bikes, hiking, playing house and other normal activities.

We had only a few stuffed animals, not beds and dressers full as my children had. It seems back then, we just had a lot less "stuff."

One year, my father, who was fun loving and extravagant by nature, went to Kessler's in Canton and bought the very biggest Easter baskets he could find for my sister, my brother and me.

They were wrapped in pastel cellophane, each in a different color, and filled to the brim with candy, little toys, coloring books, prizes and goodies. And each one had a different stuffed animal.

Mine was the biggest, because I was the oldest, and had a rabbit that had these huge ears that were almost as tall as me. They were metal wrapped in fabric and stuck out of the cellophane, because they were too large to wrap. I cherished that bunny for years, because it symbolized my father so well. His desire to shower us with gifts, even when he could least afford to, the way he met life head-on always with a smile and optimism, and his genuine love of fun.

Yes, Easter has many different levels, each of them meaningful in their own way.

Easter a Time of New Beginnings

Easter Sunday morning. We know its deep religious meaning. Those of us who miss church too often during the rest of the year make sure to attend on Easter Sunday morning. Not just to wear new clothes and see and be seen.

However far we may stray the rest of the year, we go on Easter to celebrate the most significant, the core belief of our Christian faith. We go to hear the message in word and song. We go to reaffirm our faith and to commune with our God who made that greatest of sacrifices so that we may have life everlasting.

The world seems to proclaim the news. Flowers bloom, birds sing, the grass seems greener, the skies bluer on Easter than on any day of the year.

So many tragedies mark the year. So many losses, missed opportunities, botched chances. We make our resolutions to do better, to be that person we know we can be. Somehow, Easter opens a ray of light, a beam of hope for a better tomorrow.

My daughter's college roommate is Jewish. She is coming home with my daughter for the holiday. This lovely young woman is from a devout family who treasures their religious heritage and traditions. My daughter has had a chance to visit

Hometown Holidays

in her home and share in those observances of that faith.

Now, we have a chance to share that most meaningful of religious holidays for Christians with her. That has given me pause.

She has never dyed Easter eggs, chased after a bunny or new chick, gotten up early to find out what the Easter bunny brought, put on a fancy new dress trimmed with ribbons and lace and shiny new white shoes, donned an Easter bonnet and crammed into a car after eating too many chocolate eggs to head to church

She has never attended an Easter sunrise service and seen the first rays of the sun creep into the sky, staining it pale pink, much as the sky must have looked when Mary Magdalene went to visit the tomb 2000 years ago.

She has never taken part in an Easter celebration, raising her voice loud with the strains of "Christ the Lord has risen today, hallelujah."

But she has walked the streets of Jerusalem. She has lived in the city where Jesus made His triumphant entrance, walked with His disciples, ate the Lord's Supper, was tried, found guilty, mocked in the streets and put to death on the cross.

Will she see in us the appreciation for this great sacrifice? Will she feel how much this religious celebration means to us in our hearts, how significant this passage is in our religious year and life?

Cherokee County is a community filled with churches; our roadways are dotted with places of worship. We are the buckle on the Bible belt, a community with roots deep in religious heritage. From the very beginning of our history here in this county, religion played an important role. The first preacher was appointed to an area around 1830, probably in the Sixes community. Those early preachers were few and far between. Communities often waited a long time between visits. Missionaries and Methodist circuit riders would travel from settlement to settlement spreading the good news.

They met in the open air, or in homes of the residents. As years went by, churches began to spring up. Those early residents knew what was important. They weren't worried about egg hunts or bonnets. They wanted a chance to renew their faith at the well of worship.

The religious heritage of our earliest settlers has endured. What happened 2000 years ago is fresh to us today and has been since the first settlers gathered to hear the Word.

Our greatest mystery that almost defies understanding. Our greatest triumph that promises us death shall not destroy us, but set us free.

The dogwoods are blooming and spring is here. The dark, cold of winter is over. Life is beginning again. What the world around us promises, God delivers. I may have trouble sharing how I feel about Easter, but I feel it in my heart.

Mother's Day

Rebecca and her mother on Mother's Day in 1958.

"Mother love is the fuel that enables a normal human being to do the impossible."
Marion C. Garretty

Best Days Are Mother's Days

Melanie Wilkes said the best days are the days when babies are born.

I agree.

Someone once asked me what some of the happiest experiences of my life were, and when I reflected on that question, I realized that it was the days I became a new mother.

I myself was born in Coker Hospital on Hospital Circle in Canton. The experience was a lot harder on my mother than on me.

It was right in the middle of the Dog Days of summer and a heat wave gripped North Georgia with ferociousness. The hospital was not air conditioned, since the refrigeration on large masses of air was considered an unwarranted and unheard of luxury in those days.

At our home, a small electric circular fan would stir the air in all directions on the screened porch. Mother spent most of her days there on the glider waiting to deliver her first child. She was 29 at the time and my father was 35, considered a little old to be producing offspring for the first time.

Mother and I stayed in the hospital for five days and came home in an ambulance. It wasn't that she had a particularly difficult birth. That was how things were done then.

From that day until this, my mother has dedicated her life to being the best mother she can be. She threw herself into motherhood with the grace of June Cleaver, the dedication of Mother

Theresa and the enthusiasm of Doris Day. It was her life work.

She did all the things good mothers do. She made sure we had nutritious meals at regular times, that we did our homework, didn't sit too close to the television, knew how to properly cut our meat, put our napkins in our laps, say grace, please, thank you, yes ma'am and no sir.

She signed homework, filled out offering envelopes, counted pennies, and doled out dollars for allowance.

She kept up photo albums, and saved our best homework and artwork, drove us to piano and dance lessons, washed and folded thousands of loads of clothes, ironed our cheerleading blouses and our Sunday dresses, matched our socks, combed our hair and made sure we were always dressed appropriately for every occasion.

She cheered us on when we got down, encouraged us to do our best when we wanted to slack, helped us to study, excel, go to college, and to try and make something of ourselves.

A lot of times she gave me unwanted advice I didn't want to hear, but somehow a little of it always stuck with me.

Most of all, she taught me that loving each other is more important than anything else. And that family is something to cherish and be thankful for.

And somehow, on that special day when I became a mother, what she had taught me through her example was there to pull me through. When I felt overwhelmed, or annoyed or impatient, I remembered her patience and her love.

I especially remembered how good her hands would feel holding my head when I was sick, and how she never let me down in any way.

When you bring a new life into the world, the day might be hot as blazes or colder than anything, rainy, stormy, sunny or cloudy. You might be in a big city hospital, or a small town clinic, or at home. The conditions around you don't matter.

What matters is the love you feel. The new life you begin.

It is like a chain, mother to child, down through the generations. This Mother's Day I thank my mother for all she gave me spiritually and all she taught me, and all she loved me. And I thank my own children for all that they have brought into my life.

And I remember, that mother always knows best.

Gone Before You Turn Around

The house is quiet these days, usually fairly clean, sometimes even a little orderly.

The sound of slamming doors and children's laughter, the mounds of schoolbooks and papers are all a thing of the past. Look in the refrigerator and you find only a small bottle of milk, cartons of orange juice that last for weeks and no snack foods.

This is a house where two middle-aged adults with busy jobs and busy lives reside.

This Mother's Day holds a special present for me that's both exhilarating and exciting, but also a little sad.

This spring both my children reach a milestone in their lives – they are graduating from college. That fills me with a sense of accomplishment. I feel myself bursting with pride and with joy that they are finished with their formal education and ready to move into the next stages of their lives.

It also leaves me with a flood of memories of all the wonderful years when they were under my roof and my care. It leaves me with memories of living rooms being given over to playpens and baby swings and toys. Of days of grocery lists that included baby food and diapers, of struggling to find time to just run a comb through my hair, of weeks when the only thing I really wanted was a few hours of uninterrupted sleep.

The process of becoming a mother doesn't happen when they hand you that blue or pink bundle at the hospital. That is just the beginning of a journey that lasts a lifetime - yours and theirs.

Each stage is precious. Those days of infancy when you struggle just to make sure they are fed and diapered and clothed. When you spend long hours just gazing into those little eyes that look up at you as though you are the center of the universe.

The softness of baby hair, the sweet fragrance of clean baby skin, the way that little dimpled hand wraps around your finger with a clutch that you feel all the way down into your heart.

All too quickly, they are taking their first steps, and getting their first heady taste of independence, as they run shakily away from you, gazing back with laughter in their eyes and mischief in their smile. You can still run faster, catch them up into a big hug and swing them up into the air. But not for long.

Slowly they take control, first of themselves. They can dress themselves and feed themselves. But they still need you at night to tuck them into bed, to read that one last story and hear that one last prayer. When they are hurt they want you to hold them and rock them and make them feel safe and cherished and loved.

Then in the blink of the eye they are standing with their hand on the front door, book bag on their shoulder, ready to sail forth into their own world of school and teachers and playmates.

You take their hand and walk them to school, then you feel them let go, although it is hard for them, and harder for you.

You pack their lunches, and do their laundry and help with homework. You smooth out each little crumpled piece of artwork, you admire those first attempts at writing their name, and you listen as they sound out the first words they can read.

Before long you are cheering at their ballgames, driving them to dance classes or basketball practice. You watch them stretch and seek and soar.

You are their confidant when their egos are bruised and their feelings are hurt, you share their triumphs and victories.

You're there for that first date, that first prom, that first heartbreak.

You stand on the sidelines as they grow spiritually, intellectually and socially, and then all too soon they are ordering high school graduation invitations, looking at college brochures, applying for jobs, making plans that don't include you.

The day comes when you pack up their things, watch them hop in their car and wave goodbye as they head out on their own.

Sometimes you go into their room, pick up that forgotten stuffed animal, bury your face in it and remember when they needed you more than anyone in the world.

Then you wipe the tears out of your eyes and smile to yourself, because you know they will always need you. After all, you're their mother.

Rose of Remembrance for My Mother

When I was growing up my father would always go out early in the morning on Mother's Day and come back home with red roses he had cut for us to wear to church.

He would find the roses growing on a fence on cotton mill property where he worked.

We would pin them on and wear them as we worshipped, the bright crimson spilling across our Sunday best in a joyful celebration of a mother's love. In the language of flowers red roses say I love you; worn on Mother's Day they signify your mother is alive.

Last Mother's Day I knew it would probably be my last to share with my mother in this world. In the days leading up to the special weekend to mark motherhood, my own mother had been through a series of grueling medical tests.

We did not have the results on the biopsy from the laboratory yet, but the doctors had already told us it did not look promising. My mother had a tumor that appeared malignant.

We went home to wait for the results. Although our minds had not yet accepted it, our hearts knew that things would never be the same again.

But for that one day, life was as we had always known it. We gathered around my mother's dining room table, the one where we had eaten special occasion meals all our lives.

The whole family was there, children and grandchildren. While we had a foreshadowing of what was to come, we still smiled and loved and talked and cared and ate. It was a day of celebration of a mother's love and a mother's life.

I thought that day as I always have on Mother's Day of all the good things my mother gave me, all the love she lavished on me in her own silent and strong way. My mother was not a gushy woman. But in reflecting back, I realize that showed her love was all the stronger.

She demonstrated her love, rather than talked it. She had many jobs in her life, but her career was being a mother. She dedicated herself to that responsibility and challenge with total resolve.

When we had children of our own, she continued to mother us and mother them. Making sure we ate right, studied, did our best, worked hard, kept our houses clean and our lives in order.

She was the point around which we all pivoted, the central guiding force of our day-to-day existence.

As she got up in years, she and I talked on the phone every day at least once, if not more often just to make sure she was doing all right. She was always interested in me, always loved me, was always, always there.

But last Mother's Day I knew she was preparing to leave us.

The next day we went to the doctor and from there to a hospital in Atlanta where my mother remained for 14 days to undergo a horrendous round of tests and 12 grueling hours of surgeries.

She never returned home to the house where she had lived for more than 50 years. She moved into an assisted living home, and while we all hoped she would recover and go back to her own home, we knew that was unlikely.

Throughout her illness she remained as strong as she had always been, sparing us from much of what she was going through and being so brave.

She died on Christmas Day.

As hard as it was to say goodbye and to let her go from this world, and as tough as it made Christmas, she stepped from this world to the next on a day she always loved and made wonderful for us. The day of joyous celebration of God's gift to the world.

We chose red roses for her funeral, the flowers she loved so much, that signified love and life.

She never liked white roses. I don't think I will ever wear one. Instead I will celebrate Mother's Day in quiet reflection, and perhaps stop to pick a red rose on the side of the road and drink in the fragrance that still reminds me of those happy Mother's Days long ago when we went to church and sat at our mother's side, safe and happy and protected.

Mother's Day Toothache a Sore Spot

More than 28 years ago I came home from the hospital with a little bundle that was our son Nathan.

This week I developed a toothache that reminded me of those early days of motherhood. I think of it as my Mother's Day toothache.

While the dental problem is happening now, it all started in those nights when I was a young new mother and the stress of motherhood made me grit my teeth in my sleep.

I was younger than my son is now when I had him, and up until that time I had led a carefree existence with little real responsibility. All of that was about to change.

Nathan was what they called a colicky baby and I was what they called a very inexperienced mother.

My own mother had always done everything at our home, pouring herself into motherhood with all the passion of the post-war generation. It was her calling and her full-time job.

Her three children and her husband lived in a well-run home where beds where always made, by her, clothes cleaned and neatly hung, and delicious hot meals served around the kitchen table where we all ate as a family.

She made it all seem so easy that I never realized what was really involved in her job until I had my own family.

Here I now had this wonderful little son, this beautiful baby boy who looked up at me with the most intense eyes that never left my own and I wasn't sure what exactly to do with him.

I carried him into the nursery we had so lovingly and attractively decorated with a canopy bed, Peter Rabbit wallpaper, mobiles, a rocking chair, and matching changing table. In those days we didn't know the sex of the baby before it was born, so our decorating scheme was chosen to fit either.

I showed him his room and put him down in his bed. He lay there quietly for a minute and then he began screaming bloody murder.

I picked him up and walked him and rocked him and tried to calm him. Finally he fell asleep on my shoulder, but every time he felt the bed underneath him, he would start crying again.

This continued for the next six months with me questioning my sanity, my mothering instinct and just about everything else in my life.

People told me that I was just nervous and that he was picking up my own fears and anxieties. Each visit to the pediatrician I was told he was just fine, I needed to relax.

My husband was working in downtown Atlanta, gone all day probably to his great relief. At night he was working on his master's degree and studying for his CPA exam. Still he found time to help out with the baby.

But I was usually the one who got up with the baby during the night. And when I finally got him down, I would fall into a fitful sleep and grit my teeth. One day a great big tooth broke in half and a horrible trip to the dentist followed.

Rebecca Johnston

Over the years whenever that tooth flared up again I would remember those early days of motherhood and how awfully challenged I was.

Of course after a while with the help of coffee and Dr. Spock and my own mother and my mother-in-law and several neighbors and all my friends who had children of their own and my husband I got a little bit better at the job.

And now when I look back most of the time I just remember all the good times. Rocking Nathan in the dark and feeling his little body so close to my heart.

Watching him learn to crawl, then walk. Hearing his first little words. Reading his little books to him. The days flew by all too fast and soon babyhood was over.

He was a toddler, rushing around the yard on his little toys, playing with his new baby sister, going to preschool, starting to play soccer, singing in the church choir.

Before we knew it he was going off to kindergarten, never looking back, always a little serious, loving all sports, competitive, honest, and trustworthy and a good friend to everyone. Now he is all grown up, married to a lovely young lady.

Despite my failings as a mother, he became a son we can be proud of.

Dr. Matthew Phelps is my dentist and he can confirm that while I think he is the greatest dentist in the world, I hate going to see him. I have to be one of his most nervous patients.

But as I lay awake in bed with my toothache this week, I thought about the reason I broke the tooth in the first place all those years ago. And I knew that toothache was a small pain to pay for all the joys of motherhood.

Father's Day

Jim Wheeler and Rebecca at age two.

"I cannot think of any need in childhood as strong as the need for a father's protection."
                    Sigmund Freud

Ordinary Man was Extraordinary Father

When I was a little girl I would sit on the front stoop of our house and watch for my Dad to come home from work.

The minute I saw his old car nosing up the driveway I would run as fast as I could to the bottom of the hill to get to ride up the driveway with him. He would always stop and wait, reach across the seat and open the door on the passenger's side to make room for me on the front seat no matter how crowded with his business of the day it was.

On that one minute ride up the drive I would begin to pour out to him all the small happenings of my own day and he would listen intently, never letting on that he was tired from work, ready to change out of his suit and tie and have a few minutes of well earned relaxation himself.

That is the magical, wonderful thing about loving and good fathers. They always make time for their children. They always listen. They always find room in their lives and in their hearts for us.

My father was not an extraordinary man. He was an ordinary man who gave extraordinarily to his family.

I now know with the wisdom of adulthood, that, like many dads back then and today, he must have had a lot of worries to occupy his mind over the years.

Worries about money and job and commitments to community and church that took time and involvement. Worries about his elderly mother who lived alone and depended on him for so much. Worries about how he would make ends meet from paycheck to paycheck with three small children. Worries about how he would send us all to college and help us make a successful start in the world.

But no matter how busy he was, somehow at the end of the day, he was always there for me. He shared his own interests with me. And most of all he listened.

He was never judgmental throughout my childhood and teen years. He was unfailingly kind and also proud of my accomplishments, big and small.

My father grew up here in Canton during the Depression, and like so many people in small rural towns, didn't have a lot.

His own father died when he was only 17, just two months away from high school graduation that spring of 1935.

My father worked hard the rest of his 72 years to give a good life to his family.

The dividend of his life was the joy he took in everything. He found humor and laughter wherever he looked. He loved a good joke and to pull someone's leg. He was known for being full of foolishness.

Many years have passed since I was that little girl running with pigtails flying down the hill.

In fact, it has been 15 years this weekend since my father died of cancer. He died on June 21, the longest day of the year.

In my memory, it is one of the longest days of my life, and one of the hardest. His family sat around him, knowing that he would not live much longer. Each breath he drew was hard.

He had fought a long battle and he held on to life longer than any doctor ever expected.

I know he was in pain. But I know too that each moment on this earth was precious to him. I know that even in sickness and in death he loved each of us, his family, with all his being.

On this special anniversary and on this special holiday to honor fathers I thank him in my heart for all he did for me and all he meant to me.

Father-Daughter Walk Down Memory Lane

Last week I was at an event in Woodstock and Sen. Chip Rogers showed up with his 2-year-old daughter curled up on his shoulder.

He told us that as he was getting ready to go out he mentioned that she might want to go with him and she ran to her car seat. That was good enough answer for him to bring her along.

He held her the entire meeting as he stood and chatted with the folks in attendance. She quietly gazed out at the crowd with a solemn look, her head on her daddy's shoulder. Her trust in her father was just so touching and poignant.

The sight took me back to my own childhood and my dad. He was the kind of guy who loved being involved in the community and seemed to attend a meeting just about every night of the week between church, civic clubs and politics.

At an early age I began to tag along. He was always happy to have me as company.

Our old car didn't have seat belts and I would perch myself up on the front seat beside him, excited at accompanying him to a gathering.

Some of my happiest memories are of Ladies Night at the Lion's Club. My mother would always go to the formal ones at the Pine Crest Restaurant, but she sometimes chose to stay home with the younger children when the event was an outdoor fish fry or a barbecue.

I was just as happy as a clam to go along instead.

The Canton Lions met for their summer night out with the ladies down at Field's Landing on Allatoona Lake.

The old pavilion would be lit with yellowish light spilling out into the summer twilight. Men would cook the dinner and everyone would line the long wooden picnic tables to dig into the simple fare.

Back then, everyone knew everyone in town. Events gave people a chance to catch up on what their acquaintances were doing. Time was slower, friendships were deeper, conversation was something to savor.

As the fireflies would start to come out and the speeches begin, I would sometimes wander down to the edge of the water and wade in, feeling the mud squish between my toes.

The lake would look dark and mysterious, in contrast with the warm glow behind me. Then as the evening was about to end, I would run to find my father and slip my hand in his, feeling safe and loved.

He was always so jolly as we headed home, whistling and singing old tunes from the 1940s that I remember to this day.

The time he spent with me as a child helped shape me into the person I am today.

He was always proud of his children, even though our accomplishments were fairly ordinary. Just like he loved even the simple pleasures of life like eating homemade ice cream on the Fourth of July or hiking in the woods as the leaves reached their most brilliant color or getting an unexpected post card from a friend in the mail.

Rebecca Johnston

My father was almost always cheerful. That is what I remember the most. That and how much he loved his family.

It has been 18 years since he died. His death came just a few days after Father's Day on June 21, the longest day of the year.

Of course I still miss him so much. But most of all I am so thankful for all the time we spent together, for all the times he forgave me when I got into trouble, cheered me on when I needed it, picked up the pieces when I failed.

I know I was a Daddy's girl and that when I put my hand in his, I was safe and sound in a way that no one and nothing else could make me.

Fathers like Chip Rogers who take the time to include their children, to be a part of their lives, no matter how busy or tired or stressed they are, are giving the greatest gift possible.

It is no accident that God is portrayed as our Father. Through the love our earthly fathers give us we can understand the love that God has for us.

I know that my own dad loved me with all his heart and that is something that I will cherish my entire life. I know that he always knew how much I loved him, not just on Father's Day, but every day in the ordinary times and places of life. And for that I am doubly thankful.

Fourth of July

Independence Day celebration in downtown Canton.

Freedom's natal day is here.
Fire the guns and shout for freedom,
See the flag above unfurled!
Hail the stars and stripes forever,
Dearest flag in all the world.
                    Florence A. Jones

Elvis's Limo Makes 4th King of Holidays

The summer air was heavy with humidity that Fourth of July.

I was 13 years old, standing between the days of childhood and those of being a young adult. Canton was still sleeping in relative peace. Little seemed to have changed in Cherokee County in a hundred years.

There was no threat of rampant growth or mega highways; there was little crime. The air was pure and sweet. We had never heard of El Nino. Water was plentiful.

The mills always shut down on the Fourth of July week, giving a pause in the busy, hot life of the town.

All the years of my childhood, the Fourth of July was a family event when we cooked out, decorated our bicycles and my brother's little tractor and wagon, and had a homemade parade of our own.

My father would always cook hamburgers and hot dogs, and fix ice cream floats made with Nehi grape soda poured over vanilla ice cream.

But this holiday was different. I was hanging out with friends in town for the day of activities.

And best of all, Elvis's limousine was going to make an appearance in downtown Canton.

Those were the days when most Saturday afternoons I would go to the Canton Theater to see movies that featured my favorite entertainers. If the Canton Theater showed many movies with plots, I don't remember them.

I would sit in the cool refrigerated air in the gold plush seats, giggling with my friends and listening to the Beatles, or Herman's Hermits, or some other British invasion group play their top 40 hits and wrap them around some thin story line about meeting the right girl, or being discovered.

But the best, most romantic, most scintillating movies of all were those featuring the King.

He was always in some trouble. Parents or his boss or the city leaders would fail to see just how wonderful he was. But there was always some gorgeous young lady who would champion his cause. And he would charm her, and his entire female listening audience, with the purest sweetest voice ever heard.

He might be in love with Nancy Sinatra, or maybe Ann Margaret, or some other sultry siren. But sitting in the dim light of the Canton Theater, I could imagine it was I.

So when I heard that Elvis's limousine was going to be in Canton as part of the Fourth of July festivities, I just knew I had to go.

My grandmother lived on Main Street, within walking distance of town, and that was always my base of operation for my schemes.

So I gathered up a pack of my 13-year-old friends, and we headed for the downtown area that hot and muggy July morning.

Canton went in for Independence Day in a big way. Not much else happened here all summer.

Booths were set up in the parking lot where the Cherokee County Justice Center now stands.

On the steps of the white marble courthouse, a series of local bands paraded onto the bandstand all afternoon long.

And parked right in front of the Canton Theater was Elvis's limo. Now some people might have thought that Elvis himself should have come to town that day, but even then I knew that Canton was a little small for that kind of royal visit.

For just a little while, I got to peer into the interior of his private sanctum inside a gold Cadillac outfitted like none I had ever seen.

The seats were made of white fur, and there were crystal decanters and tumblers fitted into little recesses. I could imagine my hero riding around some faraway city with some beautiful lady by his side. Laughing, talking, pouring a drink. Living the good life.

There might have been marching bands, and flags, and patriotic speeches that Fourth of July.

But what I remember is the chariot of the King, and its unlikely inclusion in Canton's celebration of our country's freedom.

Final Salute To a Good Soldier

It seems like just yesterday that I glanced up from my desk in the newsroom at the Cherokee Tribune and saw him standing there.

He was tall and thin, with a head of wavy hair. He was holding an old camera that looked like a Polaroid from another era. He asked if he could have a moment of my time and introduced himself as Bob Campbell.

He told me that he was going to be doing the publicity for the local American Legion and that he would be bringing by photos on a regular basis to submit for publication.

The year was 1988 and that was the first frame of a friendship that clicked along for almost two decades and generated a mental scrapbook of fond memories.

When you work in the media you meet all kinds of people. You become, I hate to admit it, a little jaundiced. People say they are going to do something and don't. People ask you to do something that is not possible and get offended when you have to say no. People attempt to use the media for their own ends and ambitions. But then there are the good guys.

Bob proved to be one of those good guys. For years, and I mean years, he faithfully brought in information about the American Legion. He became a really good photographer and he wrote a mean press release.

Most of all he was polite and friendly and supportive of the newspaper and grateful for any coverage.

He got us involved in all kinds of projects. Boys and Girls State, the Oratorical Contest, the Memorial Day and Veteran's Day celebrations, the Poppy Sale. The list goes on and on.

In the years of 1997 and 1998 he served as the state American Legion Commander, an extremely high honor and one indicative of his dedication, his personality and his commitment.

Bob saw active duty as a member of the United States Navy during World War II. He returned home and used the American Legion sponsored GI Bill to attend North Carolina State University to get a degree in aeronautical engineering.

After graduating in 1956 he went to work for Lockheed Aircraft Corp. as an engineer. He worked there for 32 years.

He was a member of the American Legion for 53 years and did so much in so many capacities for the organization of veterans.

Along the way he found time to do a lot of other things in the community, like serving on the Board of Directors of the Cherokee Chamber of Commerce, and serving on the Cherokee Sewerage and Water Authority.

Bob was honored in the county with awards for Volunteer of the Year from the Chamber, the Liberty Bell Award from the Cherokee County Bar Association and a host of others.

On this patriotic holiday of the birth of our nation, I am reminded of how important the men and women of Bob's generation are and have been to our country.

And how in so many ways they are a dying breed.

They survived the World War to come home and marry and enter the job market and start the baby boomers generation.

They lived lives of patriotism and family values and community service and high ethics and morals. They were proud of their country and their service to it, their families and their God.

They came through the fire and stood tall and tough like tempered steel to inspire us, to remind us.

They are good men and women and each time one falls to sickness and old age we lose a little piece of what has kept our nation strong for a very long time.

I am not sure that I have faith in my generation and the one following us to hold that standard high. Only time will tell that story. But the generation that fought World War II, now that is some kind of legacy.

Last week Bob died after a battle with cancer.

The last picture in my memories of him is at the Sept. 11, 2002, service at Sequoyah High School one year after the beginning of the present War on Terrorism.

He represented the U.S. Navy in the presentation of the colors. He wore his uniform that he had from the Navy days of World War II.

He could still fit into it. He still looked like a Navy guy out of an old movie.

And when the field band played "Anchors Away" he solemnly saluted in honor of his country.

Today I salute him.

Freedom of Religion Touches Life

I have cancer phobia.

I can't seem to help it. Watching both my parents die of cancer, coupled with a terribly vivid imagination makes my mind fertile ground for worry.

The year I graduated from Cherokee High, there was a senior superlative designation of "Most Imaginative" and I received it. I always secretly thought it was for the craziest person in the class. Maybe I deserve both designations.

As I get older, my imagination more easily runs rampant. I also seem to be getting a little crazier. When any health issues crop up, I immediately begin to imagine the worst.

Being able to easily get medical information on the internet has only compounded the problem. Whatever symptom I have I am able to find a horrible disease that fits it.

The only way to battle my phobia is through prayer. It takes a power far greater than my own to take away my fears.

Recently, I had some persistent health issues that warranted a trip to the doctor. He decided to do some tests – hateful word.

The tests were done and then the waiting began.

My doctor is Dr. Michael Litrel. He told me to call back in a week rather than wait for them to mail the results to me because he knew that I would be anxious.

Even though I worry a lot, my natural tendency is just to ignore. What I don't know won't hurt me. So I didn't want to know. Not really.

As the day when the results would be back came closer, I began to dread making that call. I really didn't know if I could make it. Better to just wait than go looking for trouble.

The day before the results were due back, as I was getting ready for work, I decided to pray about it. Not your little, "Please God, do this for me" prayer. A real, get down on your knees and humble yourself before the Lord prayer.

I prayed for a long time, about a lot of things. When I was finished I felt better, refreshed, calm, ready to face whatever was out there.

I finished getting ready for work and started out the door, grabbing my cell phone on my way out. I saw that I had some messages on the phone.

The first message was from Dr. Litrel. He had called a day early because the test results were back. He wanted to put my mind at rest and to tell me that the results came back all right, nothing was wrong. I was to see him again in a couple of months.

The time of his call was exactly when I was praying to God.

As I thanked God for hearing my prayers, I thought about all the things I have to be thankful for, my family, my friends, my job, my health, my country, my freedom to worship God.

I talk a lot about the First Amendment freedoms, but I don't often talk about freedom of religion. That is an area where I don't have much real expertise.

But on this weekend when we celebrate the freedoms we enjoy in our country, I just want to say how glad I am that we can worship God as we want.

Many of our forefathers came here fleeing religious persecution. They founded our country on some lofty principles that are often difficult to uphold.

But clearly in black and white our Bill of Rights grants freedom of religion first and foremost, followed by freedom of speech, the press, assembly and petition.

That we enjoy these rights by birth should never be taken for granted.

When the fireworks go off this Fourth of July, I am going to celebrate all the freedoms our wonderful country has to offer. And most of all our freedom to thank God and worship Him for what He has given us.

Halloween

Rebecca always loved carving the family Jack O' Lantern.

"Tis the very witching time of night."
William Shakespeare

Father's Birthday More Treat Than Trick

My father was born in the yellow house on the corner of Shipp Street and East Main Street in Canton.

I don't mean that is where his parents lived when he was born. I mean his mother gave birth to him right there in that house.

My grandmother would often tell me the story of that day. She would assure me that babies were born at home as a matter of course in those days. There was nothing odd about her not going to the hospital.

The date of my father's birth was Oct. 31, 1917.

Gran always told me that the goblins brought him. He was a Halloween baby. I think it was no accident that when he was 18 years old, he was chosen the most mischievous by his senior class at Canton High School. He was always up to something, and he came by it naturally.

My grandmother was the most ladylike person. My strongest memory of her is her sitting in her front bedroom in a rocker reading the Bible and listening to the religious programming on WCHK radio station.

I never heard her raise her voice or get angry or upset. She was always kind and loving and, well, just a little Southern lady.

The thought of her in labor in her bedroom all day is a little bit much for me. We never talked about things like that. All things surrounding the actual birth itself were a mystery to me, and something about which she would just purse her mouth and shake her head if I questioned her.

But she would tell me how the doctor stayed there all day. His buggy was parked in front of the house and that is how the neighbors knew a new baby was being brought into the world. Main Street was not even paved at the time, and almost no one had a car in Canton.

The doctor was Dr. Harbin. I remember that and I looked it up in the history of Cherokee County. Sure enough, he is there. Dr. Samuel Richard Harbin, born in 1873 in Cherokee County, the son of Jephthat Harbin, who was also born in Cherokee County in 1838 and served in the Confederate Navy aboard a sailing ship. He is listed as a prominent farmer. He was married to Mary Jane Freeze, who came here from North Carolina.

Their son, Samuel, attended Atlanta Eclectic Medical College and practiced medicine for many years in Cherokee County. For the last 20 years before his death in 1932, he was a leading physician of Canton. He also was a member of the First Baptist Church of Canton.

Dr. Harbin married Montaree Bell of Ball Ground. They had six children of their own, Ethel, Stella, Otis, Tillman, Wallace and Jeffie.

My father was my grandmother's third and last child. Perhaps having the doctor's buggy at the house all day just did her in. Whatever her reason, the Halloween baby was her last and she doted on him for the next 60 years.

My Aunt Elizabeth was seven at the time my father was born. She was sent up the street to my grandmother's cousin, Fanny Bell, for the day. But she could see that buggy parked there in front of her house, and she fretted and questioned what was going on.

Finally, at just about dark, they got word the birth was a success and walked her home. They carried her in and she saw her new brother for the first time. She looked at him lying peacefully in his crib and quickly informed everyone that she was not going to look after him.

But I am sure she did. Family in those days was important. Even a baby dropped off by the goblins on Halloween got a lot of care and respect.

Canton was a close-knit community. Neighbors cared about neighbors, families helped out other families. Times were simple, but good.

The doctor could spend his day at one house delivering a baby. I am sure his pay was very small.

And my father turned out to be as much of a treat as a trick. He has been dead for almost 15 years, but on Halloween I can always see that special sparkle in his eye that meant he was up to something mischievous.

Two Clowns, But Only One Winner

All Hallows Eve - a night when the dead rise up and search for their homes, when witches celebrate and regular folks stay close by hearth and home.

Only, the witches and the skeletons and the ghosts are children enjoying their trick or treat outings, and the rest of us love to decorate with pumpkins, apples, and symbols of the harvest season.

Halloween has its dark roots in the ancient history of Great Britain and France and the Celts who once lived there. When they were conquered and became Christians, pagan celebrations were forgotten. All Saints Day was begun on November 1 as a day to honor the dead. And our present day Halloween was carved out as a night to remember the old customs.

For me, Halloween was always a sweet time, marked by lots of candy and fun. Growing up, I loved the Halloween carnival at the old gymnasium behind the school on Academy Street in Canton where I attended elementary school. That school at one time was the Canton High School, where students from all over the county came together to complete their high school education.

By the time I came along, the new Cherokee High was open, and Canton Elementary School occupied the buildings in town. Grades one through three were in the building on the right and grades four through eight were across the street in the building where the auditorium is.

But the old gym still served the school as it had for decades. On those boards, great basketball players pounded down court and fought battles for championships. By the time I was there, it was reserved for seventh and eighth-grade games. But the high bleachers, the shiny wood floor and the legacy of basketball as queen of Cherokee County sports continued.

But each fall, for one night, the gym was transformed into a carnival to delight those of all ages.

I always looked forward with great anticipation to dressing up in costume, and being dropped off by my parents for an evening of games and talk with my friends. Few parents attended, the gym was always swirling with groups of youngsters trying for prizes and laughing and talking.

Afterward, we would leave the warm, brightly lit confines of the gym and walk up Main Street in loud rowdy gangs, in search of homes where we could ring the doorbell and fill our bags with candy. Those were the days before people feared each other. While we knew most of the families along Main Street, there were a few where we would walk a little more cautiously up the walk, ring the doorbell and wait for an answer.

And there were some in which the lights were out, the leaves were rustling in the wind and no one was invited in. We would walk quickly past those in case a real witch lived there. Or sometimes, we would play a little trick, like hiding the doormat, if we were feeling really brave and full of mischief.

One year, my friend Jeannie Lathem Adams and I decided to dress alike as clowns. My grandmother had some professional costumes my cousins from Newnan had worn in some play, and we were the right size to fit into them. We grabbed them up and headed to her house where her older sisters, Nancy and Sally, helped us complete our looks. We decided Jeannie would be the fat clown, with pillows stuffed around her middle to round her out, and I would be the thin clown. We then sat around the dressing table to make up for the evening.

That dressing table is one of my preadolescent favorite memories. It was one of those elaborate skirted affairs with a glass top. Fascinating jars and compacts and bottles of makeup and perfume decorated the top. I would love to sit there and finger the different containers.

But this night, the sisters helped make us up and we headed out to the old gym.

We had fun all evening. I remember sitting up high in the bleachers, looking through our grab bags at our treats. Then the time came to announce the winners of the Best Costume contest.

To my amazement, they called the name of my friend Jeannie and she went forward to get her silver dollar and have her picture made.

I could not believe it. There we were dressed alike in my costumes and she won! Where was justice?

But somehow I swallowed my disappointment, almost, and let her know I was happy for her. We made our way out into the crisp autumn air, leaving behind the laughter and crowds and lights, and started another night of trick or treating.

In these days when terror has a new meaning and there is so much to be afraid of, those times seem doubly sweet and simple.

Thanksgiving

Kiwanis holiday dinner in 1953 at the Canton Hotel.
Photo courtesy of Cherokee County Historical Society

"There is one day that is ours. There is one day when all we Americans who are not self-made go back to the old home to eat saleratus biscuits and marvel how much nearer to the porch the old pump looks than it used to. Thanksgiving Day is the one day that is purely American."

O. Henry

Plenty to be Thankful For

My husband and I don't agree on much, but the one thing we always see eye to eye on is our love of Cherokee County.

That doesn't mean we are always in concurrence on issues that plague our growing county. Indeed, far from it. Issues like land use, road improvements, zoning restrictions can divide any two people who find themselves in debate about what is happening right now in our community. Finding a consensus among residents is a daunting task.

But as I ride around the county this Thanksgiving holiday, I see so many things that I love. Trucks hauling loads of hay, horses and cows grazing peacefully in their pastures, ponds glistening in the late fall light.

I see families playing touch football on their front lawns and children shooting hoops in their driveways.

I notice old farmhouses that have stood their place for many years and new subdivisions springing up all along the highways of our county. So many new subdivisions, that it seems more cannot possibly be crowded in, but I know they will be.

I drive past a bumper crop of new shopping strips filled with grocery stores, wondering how we can possibly consume all the food sold at all the new outlets. I see new convenience stores and fast food restaurants cropping up all across the landscape.

I see churches everywhere. All my life I have been amazed and proud of the number of houses of worship that mark the Cherokee County landscape. Small wooden buildings, larger brick facilities, all opening their doors this holiday season to welcome their members and offer them food for the soul.

I drive by MUST Ministries and I see lines of people standing in the chill of the morning waiting for a chance to pick up a basket of food to feed their hungry children this Thanksgiving.

I see volunteers working tirelessly to unload supplies and get them ready for those in need.

I see assisted living and nursing homes filled to capacity with the elderly and family members driving up to see their loved ones this holiday.

I see school pageants and church programs filled with little children singing of thanksgiving and plenty.

I think about our founding fathers who fought their way through the wilderness, looking for a better life for their families. I imagine what they thought when they rode into the fertile lands along the Etowah River and in sheltered areas such as the Salacoa Valley. My mind draws pictures of the delight they must have felt when they saw the tall pines, the mountains, the streams. They were in a place where deer and wildlife abounded, where fish were easy to catch, where they could feed their families and fill their table with the bounty of the land.

Much has changed and much remains the same since those hearty men and women came here more than 170 years ago.

Change is hard, but I think they would be pleased with the Cherokee County they find today. Yes, it is crowded, but I am glad so many want to make our community their home. I think most of us agree, just as my husband and I do.

We in Cherokee County have a lot to be thankful for.

Pumpkin Pie Recipe Stirs Up Memories

Thanksgiving is always one of my favorite observances during the year. Some years I have more to be thankful for, others less, but always it is a time to pause and count the many blessings we have.

This year with dire economic news here in Cherokee County many are beginning to wonder what the future holds. Headlines that some of the county's most respected builders and developers are facing tough financial times have a lot of people worried.

Reports about the growing number of folks living in Cherokee County who need assistance from local organizations to put food on their tables underscores the concerns.

But one of the wonderful things we have to be thankful for here in our community is that there are always people willing to help, to reach out and lend a hand when needed.

The very reason I love Thanksgiving as a holiday is that it is all about giving thanks for what we have, not what we want or desire or feel the need to buy for ourselves or others.

This quintessential American holiday has through the generations stood for family and friendship and sharing. The Pilgrims and the

Indians came up with the theme and it still holds true today.

They made do with the ingredients at hand and so can we. For those of us born Southern our legacy is getting by with what is available.

From the days following the War Between the States to the days leading up to World War II, Southerners suffered through many tough times. But they always found something to be thankful about.

I think about my own dad growing up on Main Street in Canton and coming of age during the Great Depression. I know that those years were lean.

There might not have been a big, juicy turkey, but there was at least a chicken caught out back and killed and roasted for Thanksgiving dinner.

Sweet potatoes and green beans and squash were plentiful. Southern cooks are renowned for taking those ordinary vegetables and dressing them up into fancy dishes.

I imagine that Southern cornbread dressing itself grew out of necessity. Cornmeal was much more plentiful in the South than wheat flour, and cheaper too.

Cherokee County's streams were the home of many grist mills where corn could be ground into meal and then used through the long winter to put something on the table.

So it just seemed natural to season it up with some broth and sage and crumble in a few left over biscuits and moisten it with a few eggs from the henhouse.

Cranberries weren't a local thing, so I imagine a lot of people made do with some homemade applesauce as a side dish.

But no matter how needy, Southern cooks always prided themselves on their pies. Pecan and apple, made from ingredients on hand, and especially pumpkin pies.

Farmers and even town folks with a garden out the back door could grow a few pumpkins. Although my grandparents lived in town, they hailed from the farm, and they always had a little garden near the kitchen.

My grandmother made the most delicious pumpkin pies. Even today we use her recipe at Thanksgiving.

No canned pumpkin will do. No thank you. It has to be made from a fresh pumpkin. Until my mother died I always ate pumpkin pie, but I had never made one.

The first Thanksgiving I had to cook the entire dinner I called my sister who lives in North Carolina in a panic. How do you make Mother's pumpkin pie?

Fortunately she, an avid pumpkin pie lover, had gotten the recipe and it was only then that I found out it was my grandmother's too.

You have to find a pie pumpkin, not a Halloween pumpkin. A little sweet sugar pumpkin is what is needed.

Cut it in half and remove all the seeds and yucky stuff. Place the pumpkin face down on a baking sheet and put is a 325 degree oven for an hour or so until the pumpkin is tender or begins to fall apart.

Then scrap out the pulp and discard the shells. Mash the pulp. Mix in one stick melted butter, ¾ cup sugar and cool. I add just a little milk, not much. That is my change to the recipe. When the mixture is cool, stir in one beaten egg and cinnamon and allspice to taste. Pour it into a pie shell and bake for 55 minutes at 325 degrees. Serve warm.

That is my grandmother, Belle Cochran Wheeler's recipe, and it is delicious, I promise.

Thanksgiving is about finding something to be grateful for in the ordinary. Thanksgiving is about having made it through another year with family and friends. Thanksgiving is about sharing what we have, no matter how much or how little that is.

Thanksgiving is when we as a community, and as a nation, all pause on the same day to give thanks. And that truly is a marvelous thing.

Let's Be Thankful For All We Have

If there is any community in the world that has a lot to be thankful for, it is Cherokee.

Sure we have our problems, our squabbles, and our minor disagreements. But when you get right down to it, we are one of the most fortunate counties in one of the most beautiful states in the greatest country in the world.

I am so thankful that I live in a place where I am free to worship as I wish, speak out on matters whenever I want and write in this column whatever opinion I have without fear of censorship.

I am so thankful that we have good doctors, and a good hospital like Northside Hospital Cherokee, where we can receive caring treatment for our health concerns. I am happy for each day that I and my family enjoy good health.

I am so thankful for all our churches, our pastors and lay leaders.

I am so thankful for our wonderful schools, our dedicated teachers, our school board and school Superintendent Dr. Frank Petrizello. We may have some overcrowding, we may need more new schools than we can fund, but the staff in each school gives their all each and every day for the education of our children.

I am thankful for our law enforcement and fire officials, those dedicated men and women who keep us safe in our beds each night, who are willing to put their lives on the line for our welfare and peace of mind.

I am thankful for Sheriff Roger Garrison and our city police chiefs around our county who set a standard of professional conduct.

I am thankful for all the military personnel from our community who are willing to serve our country and help keep it free and safe for all of us. I am especially thankful for those men and women who are willing to serve on foreign soil during this time of war, and for their families. They are in my prayers as they stand on the outposts of the world.

I am thankful for our court system, our judges and our attorneys and our rights under our Constitution.

I am thankful for our media, for Barbara Jacoby and the hard working writers of the Cherokee Tribune, and for all our reporters who strive to keep us informed of the events in our community.

I am thankful for the natural beauty of our community, the trees, the mountains, lakes, rivers and streams.

I am thankful for our elected officials, our mayors and city officials, our county commissioners, our state representatives and senator for their great service to our community. Although I may not agree with each and every one all the time, I know each is striving to do what he or she believes is truly best for our community.

I am thankful for the Cherokee County Arts Center and all the cultural opportunities in our community.

I am thankful for our wonderful Chamber of Commerce and Pam Carnes, our dedicated chamber executive.

Rebecca Johnston

I am thankful for all our civic organizations, our volunteers, who do such an outstanding job and are always ready to pitch in whenever needed.

I am thankful for my friends, who brighten my days so much, who are always there when I need them.

I am thankful for my wonderful husband Harry, and my two now grown-up children, Nathan and Ann.

I am thankful for our heritage, our history, our diversity and our differences that make us the community we are today.

I am thankful for all the laughter, all the fellowship, good food and times that I have shared with so many of you through the years.

As we bow our heads this Thanksgiving and give thanks, I hope we all reflect on how lucky we are to live in Cherokee County in the state of Georgia in the United States of America among the absolutely best folks anywhere around.

Memories Best Seasoning for Feast

This morning a wild turkey was standing in my driveway off Main Street in Canton.

No, I was not hallucinating, and I had not drunk too much muscadine wine last night.

There it was - a tall dark bird with a thin long neck and lanky legs. It ran harem scarem into the woods at what I suppose was a turkey trot when I tried to approach it.

In all the years I have lived here in Cherokee County that is the first wild turkey I have seen in my front yard. I was both amazed and delighted. Amazed at the reminder of finding the *piece de resistance* for your holiday meal wandering out in the woods, and delighted that we still have enough woods around us in our rapidly sprawling community to sustain a proper Thanksgiving fowl.

For most of us, tradition is the main dish at Thanksgiving dinner.

Over the generations and the years each of us carves out a menu that has special meaning just to us. That has been going on since the first Pilgrims set foot in Georgia and met up with some Indians along the Etowah River and decided to simmer up a feast of delectable morsels native to the area.

Rebecca Johnston

My family's Thanksgiving fare is stuck like a broken Frank Sinatra record in the 1950s. We love casseroles. I now pull out a total of eight 9x13 Pyrex dishes in which to cook our traditional dinner.

This year I used three pounds of butter. Now please note that our extended family and friends adds up to a meager eight souls around the groaning board.

But what makes our meal special, and I wager that it is what makes yours special too, is all the memories that bubble up along with the cranberry sauce.

This is the first year that I cooked the entire Thanksgiving meal by myself. Since my mother's death two years ago, I have avoided this moment. But finally it was here.

I had to make the dressing.

Southerners love their dressing. Forget stuffing. A proper dressing is like a soufflé of earthy smells that evokes memories of Thanksgivings past.

First you must make perfect cornbread from which to construct the perfect dressing. I pulled out the shortening for the first time in a year. I don't even know where I got it or why, but it does keep well.

Then, the black skillet was next. The only way to get cornbread to brown up properly is to use a perfectly seasoned black iron skillet. In my family well seasoned black iron cooking utensils are handed down from generation to generation with more appreciation than diamonds.

You have to melt the shortening in the skillet in the oven, then pour it into the batter and stir it all sizzling back into the pan.

Two pones of cornbread later and I was ready for the next step. Boiling the chicken. It is not enough that I have to cook a large turkey the next day. I now have to first boil a chicken to make broth to make proper dressing.

Finally, after a day and a half of cooking I had the ingredients ready for the dressing. Now, I could pull out my mother's huge mixing bowl that is big enough for the dressing and start working the ingredients into the right consistency. You mix the cornbread, broth and other ingredients until "They feel right." Then you pour them into a casserole and cook at a high heat until brown.

All of this literally stressed my cooking abilities to their limits.

But it was all worth it. When the plates were all piled high, and everyone took a taste the words that I longed to hear were uttered.

"This is the best dressing ever."

I don't even have the heart to tell you about the pumpkin pie. In our family we don't use canned pumpkin. At least we no longer grow our own.

Thanksgiving is still my favorite holiday. But since I became the one to cook the dinner it got a whole lot harder to fully appreciate.

I sometimes think about adding some nouvelle dish. But then I think back to all those years around my mother's Thanksgiving table and I give thanks that our family cooked up its own set of traditions that I can pass on down to the next generation.

Thanksgiving Cooks Up Special Feelings

Thanksgiving is in many ways my favorite holiday.

Our commercial society, tarnished by love of things, has made Christmas into something less bright than it should be, and in the process Thanksgiving has become a prelude to sales, a mark on the calendar to indicate the Christmas season is in full swing. Recently, as stores put out their Christmas merchandise around the first of October, and decorations appear before the leaves have even turned, Thanksgiving gets even less respect.

Make no mistake. I love Christmas, too. I love the bustle, the packages, the decorations, the parties. I love the sacred aspects, the quiet times around the fire, the family traditions, and the warmth of Christmas.

I just wish Christmas were a little less commercial. Thanksgiving is still stark, almost bare of ornamentation, a reflection on the harsh and humble beginnings of our country, a look at the basic necessities of life.

Thanksgiving deserves our respect. It is the day when family and friends gather just to give thanks for another year, to reflect on what is really meaningful in their lives and to look ahead to the future. It is a pause in our busy, stressful lives.

Of course, that food is a major ingredient of Thanksgiving might be another reason why I love it so.

Thanksgiving comes at a time of year I love. The leaves are almost gone, the trees bare, the sunlight thinning. The days are shortening; the squirrels are scurrying to make sure they are ready for winter. We are drawing in to hearth and home.

Thanksgiving is a time of touching each other in a special way. I remember with clarity the last Thanksgiving my father was at the table. We knew he had cancer and that it could be his last holiday with his family.

I remember the next Thanksgiving without him, the one when my sister announced she was expecting a baby the next spring, somehow helping heal our family's broken hearts.

I remember the times when my husband and I were dating, hurrying from one big meal to another in an attempt to please all the families and have time with everyone. Somehow we always made it everywhere and still got to Atlanta that evening for the lighting of the big tree at Rich's.

I remember all the years when my children were young and we made the journey to my mother's house to feast on what we always believed was the best dressing in the world.

I remember when we started having the dinner at my house, and I felt almost like a grownup because I could cook the turkey. But my mother still makes the dressing, and we still praise it as the best we have ever tasted each and every Thanksgiving.

Now my children are both in college, and Thanksgiving marks a time to draw them back home. Between cramming for exams and traveling up north to see if there is any snow for snowboarding, they promise to make time to sit down around our table and pause with family and friends to give thanks for all we enjoy in our lives.

This year is especially precious. Never in my lifetime have we as a nation been at war at Thanksgiving. With clouds of fear and uncertainty all around us, with the core of our lives shaken by the events this past September, all of us should realize more than ever how precious life is.

I think about those who have lost their loved ones this past year, those whose family members were victims of terrorism. I am filled with thanksgiving and also with heartache.

Let's make time out of our hectic lives this Thanksgiving to remember what is really important in life. Hope you have a great one.

Love of Family Has Place at the Table

When my children were young I asked my little five-year-old daughter to help me make Thanksgiving place cards for the holiday table.

Together we cut out little white paper tents and she carefully wrote out the names of different family members on each one with a little help from mom. Then my little artist drew an appropriate picture for each place card; a turkey on a platter on one, the Mayflower on another, a Pilgrim here, an Indian there.

When we were almost done her seven-year-old brother came bounding into the room to see what was going on. With a nose a little out of joint, he said that he wanted to help. In a peace offering in the war of rival siblings, my daughter said he could decorate the back side of the place cards.

Not to be outdone by a girl, he grabbed up the crayons and began to write each person's name, again, on the other side and draw his own Thanksgiving art. Unfortunately he was not the artist that his little sister was, and his turkey looked like it was levitating off the platter, his Mayflower listed badly and his Pilgrim looked more like a penguin.

But over the years those little homemade scraps of paper have become our most treasured

Thanksgiving tradition. Each year we bring them out and place them around the table.

In the 20 years that have gone by since then many things have changed in our family. Some members are no longer with us; new ones have joined our table.

One Thanksgiving my father was diagnosed with cancer and by the next year he had died.

On that first holiday without him we were given the happy announcement that my sister was pregnant for the first, and as it turned out, the only time. By the next year niece Audrey had joined our family.

Some years we can't all get together because of time and distance. But we bring out the place cards of the ones who can get there and we make new ones for those joining us for the first time.

My son is bringing his fiancé to our Thanksgiving dinner this year and by next holiday time they will be married.

This year my daughter's friend, Courtney Cook, who is battling cancer, will be with us on this special day to give thanks.

Our Rotary student, Simon Wells from Scotland, as well as two other foreign exchange students attending Reinhardt, is coming to experience the traditional Thanksgiving feast with our family.

I used to rail over the way Thanksgiving sort of got pushed to the side by Christmas. I longed for the days when we didn't see decorations going up in stores until after Thanksgiving, when the first Christmas carol was not heard until after the trimmings were turned into leftovers.

But I've mellowed. I have come to accept that we are going to start Christmas at Halloween, or maybe even Labor Day. And maybe we need that warm feeling that the holidays bring so badly that it is OK to start early.

Maybe we just can't celebrate God and family and life enough.

The grandchildren called my parents Mom Vern and Papa Jim, and every year at this time I get out their little place cards and feel their presence and their legacy.

My parents always gave me so much love, but they also taught me about what is really important in life. My father's philosophy was that we were as good as anybody, but we weren't better than anybody either. That each person should be respected no matter where they were in life and that you should give a hand to those in need and hope when you were in need someone would do the same for you.

He believed that being humble, grateful for what you have and caring for others is the spice of life. And that family is the salt that seasons everything else.

And my mother, well, she always kept me honest about myself. The other night I got out her old black Dutch oven to cook in. I was all proud of myself, flitting around the kitchen, thinking how pleased she would be of me. Suddenly, for just one second, my arm brushed the top of the pot and I burned myself.

In that instance, I could hear my mother's voice telling me to stop thinking about myself and keep my mind on what I was doing. I know that she will be watching over me as I take on that dreaded chore of cooking the dressing. She will purse her lips and shake her head that I am using bought chicken broth instead of stewing a chicken and making my own, and she will be sure to think I am putting in way too much sage.

Most of all, though, the lesson she taught me was to respect family and tradition.

Rebecca Johnston

This year when we find our little homemade place cards that mark our seats, when we sit down to dinner and bow our heads, it will be to give thanks for families, for our friends and our loved ones, here and far, and for the bounty that we enjoy in this great nation under God.

Thanksgiving Delivers A Day of Blessings

Can it be possible? Was it really 21 years ago that my daughter Ann made her way into this world? When I string all my Thanksgivings together and run them through my memory, smooth and round like pearls slipping between my fingers, each one has special memories.

The cast changes as family and friends come and go. There are sad Thanksgivings, like the year we knew my father was dying of cancer and he would not be back with us the next holiday season. And there are many, many joyous Thanksgivings, although none more special and more unique than the year Ann was born.

Ann was delivered by Caesarean section on Nov. 23, 1981, the Wednesday before Thanksgiving at Piedmont Hospital. She weighed six pounds, 12 ounces and of course was the sweetest baby I had ever seen.

Those were the days before sonograms made it easy to know the sex of the baby, so like all mothers back in those days, I had no idea whether I was having a girl or a boy. As I fought my way out of the fog of anesthesia, I could hear someone saying from what seemed like a long distance, "You have a healthy, perfect baby girl." Happiness suffused me and the pain miraculously melted away.

Rebecca Johnston

We already had a son, almost two years old. And while I had decided with my brain that I would be happy either way, my heart wanted a daughter because I knew this would be my last baby.

That Thanksgiving, I lay there in my hospital bed, staring out into the gray sky and barren trees, filled with thankfulness for the miracle of my new child. Hospitals on holidays are often dreary places. Only a few unlucky staff members roam the halls checking on patients.

That Thanksgiving afternoon passed quietly. A tray with one of those appetizing hospital meals of sliced turkey and what they considered a close proximity to the trimmings appeared. I ate a little, but what I waited for, and longed for, was a visit from my daughter.

They brought her in, all clean and sleepy, wrapped tightly in a little blanket, lying in a glass cart. Then my husband arrived with my son, looking solemn and serious, ready for a glimpse of his new baby sister.

Our family was together, complete. This year is different. This year my daughter will be far away on Thanksgiving, a stranger in a strange land. She is spending the year abroad, studying in a country where our special day of thanks is not celebrated. She tells me that many people across the pond the pilgrims sailed many years ago do not like Americans. That they see us as arrogant warmongers, sated on our power and wealth.

With the shadow of terrorism casting a pall over the world, with evil laying an icy finger on the backs of our necks and with the threat of war hanging in the air, sometimes we wonder where it is all leading.

We think back to the brave few who left their families to sail to a new world where men dreamed of freedom, of the ability to worship, bear arms, tell the truth and be equal. Despite what is going on in the world, this Thanksgiving, like so many through the centuries before it, is a time when we can count our blessings.

Each of us knows what Thanksgiving means personally to us. To each of you I wish a blessed day.

About The Author

Newspaper columnist and local writer Rebecca Johnston is a Cherokee County native and former managing editor of the Cherokee Tribune. For more than a decade in the 1980s and 1990s she was a reporter and editor at the county newspaper. For the last eight years she has been a local columnist for the Cherokee Tribune and has won several Georgia Press Association awards for her writing, including the 2007 First Place Award for Serious Columnist. Growing up in the Canton of the 1960s flavors her writings with a wonderful sense of times past. A graduate of Cherokee High School and the University of Georgia, during her career she has also hosted local radio shows and appeared on cable television news and programming. She and her husband, Harry Johnston, live in historic Canton. They have two grown children, Nathan and Ann.

Printed in the United States
130370LV00002B/3/P